The Urbana Free Library

To renew: call 217-367-4057
or go to *urbanafreelibrary.org*
and select "My Account"

The Renaissance
INVENTORS

With
**HISTORY
PROJECTS**
for Kids

Alicia Z. Klepeis

Nomad Press
A division of Nomad Communications
10 9 8 7 6 5 4 3 2 1

This book was manufactured by Friesens Book Division
Altona, MB, Canada
October 2018, Job #246313

ISBN Softcover: 978-1-61930-685-1
ISBN Hardcover: 978-1-61930-683-7

Educational Consultant, Marla Conn

Questions regarding the ordering of this book should be addressed to
Nomad Press
2456 Christian St.
White River Junction, VT 05001
www.nomadpress.net

Printed in Canada.

Titles in *The Renaissance for Kids* Series

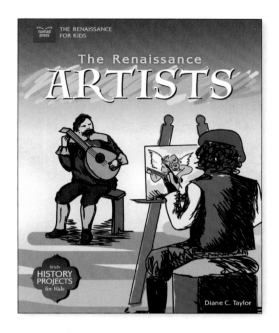

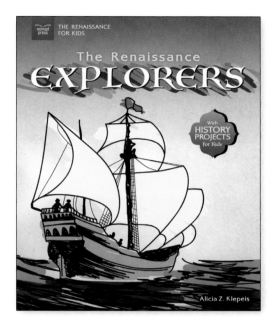

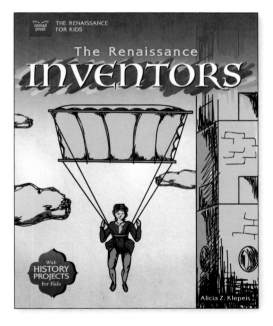

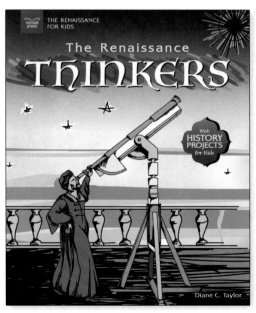

TABLE OF
Contents

GALILEO GALILEI

38. HOMO VOLANS.

Homo Volans
An illustration
by Faust Vranci⟨c⟩
showing an earl⟨y⟩
parachute of hi⟨s⟩
own design, bas⟨ed⟩
on the work of
Leonardo da Vin⟨ci⟩

INVENTION DURING THE
Renaissance

The Vitruvian Man by Leonardo da Vinci is a study of the proportions of the human body. It was drawn around 1490.

Imagine setting up a secret workshop where you try to create an invention unknown to humankind. Or staying up late to look at the stars and planets to figure out how the universe works. Or designing vehicles hundreds of years before they are actually built. These were just some of the things that inventors did during the Renaissance.

FAST FACTS

WHAT:
THE RENAISSANCE, A HISTORICAL ERA MARKED BY DRAMATIC CHANGE

WHEN: 1300s–1600s

WHERE:
ITALY AND NORTHERN EUROPE

The Renaissance is one of history's most important periods. It took place between the 1300s and the 1600s. The Renaissance began in Florence, Italy, during the fourteenth century and spread north to places as far away as England.

> "In [Nature's] inventions nothing is lacking, and nothing is superfluous."
>
> **LEONARDO DA VINCI**

What was the Renaissance really about? The word *renaissance* means "rebirth." The word is used to refer to the rebirth or renewal of interest in learning—about art, architecture, science, literature, and other fields of study.

During this time, there was also a great renewal of interest in studying ancient Greece and Rome. Many Renaissance leaders had been born in Italy's city-states. These people often found inspiration in the civilizations of ancient Greece and Rome.

Renaissance Invention
1300s–1600s

1340s–50s
The bubonic plague kills tens of millions of people across Europe, one-third of its population.

1452
Artist and inventor Leonardo da Vinci is born.

1455
The Gutenberg Bible is printed in Mainz, Germany.

1508–12
Italian artist Michelangelo paints the ceiling of the Sistine Chapel.

You can still visit these ancient Roman ruins today.

From Hard Times to New Discoveries

The Renaissance came after the Middle Ages, which had been a tough time for ordinary people. Peasants worked in the fields from sunrise to sunset and had no time or freedom to pursue their interests. They did not own their land and, despite working hard, were very poor.

○ **1510–14**	○ **1517**	○ **1522**	○ **1570**	○ **1608**	○ **1610**
Polish astronomer Nicolaus Copernicus puts forth his heliocentric theory, that the sun—not the earth—is the center of the universe.	Martin Luther protests against the Catholic Church, starting the movement known as the Reformation.	The first circumnavigation of the globe, begun by Ferdinand Magellan's fleet, is completed by Juan Sebastian Elcano.	The world's first atlas is published by Flemish cartographer Abraham Ortelius.	The telescope is invented by Hans Lippershey.	Galileo Galilei discovers the four moons of Jupiter.

3

An engraving of Johannes Gutenberg, who invented the printing press and made books available to many more people

By Nicolas de Larmessin, sixteenth century

Hardly anyone in the Middle Ages was able to read. Books were not common because they were all written by hand, and most of them were written in Latin. This is a language that only the most educated people understood. With Johannes Gutenberg's invention of the printing press, books became more common.

As people learned to read and became more aware of the world around them, they began to want a better way of life. People traveled farther from the small villages in which they were born and raised, and discovered a whole world waiting for them.

The Renaissance was a great period of trade and economic growth. People of all types had a chance to get rich, or at least financially secure, through hard work. When people didn't have to worry about starving, they had the time to think about new inventions and ideas. The Renaissance was a period of brilliant, groundbreaking new discoveries.

The brains of Renaissance thinkers seemed to explode with incredible ideas. In both philosophy and science, people came to be thought of as the center of the universe. Thinking about men and women from thousands of years ago and wondering about their lives led many of these people to be curious about human beings in their own time.

WONDER WHY?

What past civilizations do you feel inspired by? Why?

Life on the farm during the early 1500s
Workshop of the master of James IV of Scotland, fifteenth to sixteenth century

This way of thinking is called humanism. It was a new, radical idea. Men and women in the Renaissance were very religious, and the Catholic Church was a powerful force in the world and in people's lives. But more and more, people began to trust their own senses and experiences to understand how the world worked.

New Technology

During the Renaissance, creative, curious people dove into investigating how things worked. Scientists and inventors experimented and tinkered. They came up with new inventions and discoveries.

> **"I want to be a Renaissance woman. I want to paint, and I want to write, and I want to act, and I want to just do everything."**
>
> **EMMA WATSON (1990–), ACTRESS**

Many brilliant minds pursued knowledge during the Renaissance. Some became explorers and traveled around the world. Some studied math and science. Others focused on art and architecture. In addition to learning about these things, people also expanded European knowledge by creating new inventions.

This fit in perfectly with the Renaissance emphasis on innovation. Some of the inventions created during this period reflect the cutting-edge science of the time.

Have you ever used a telescope to look at the stars and planets? During the Renaissance, people improved this tool so they could peer into the exciting realm of space. Then, looking inward instead of outward, scientists used the compound microscope to look at tiny things so small they couldn't be seen with the naked eye.

MUSIC TO OUR EARS

Do you play the violin, viola, or cello? All three of these instruments were invented during the Renaissance! Around 1550, these instruments appeared in northern Italy, particularly in the cities of Cremona and Brescia. A man named Andrea Amati was part of the first generation of instrument makers to add a fourth string to violins. It was mainly professionals who played these instruments. Small groups of musicians, known as consorts, were often made up of a cello, two violas, and a violin. These groups were hugely popular and were known for playing instrumental music for people to dance to.

Listen to music that might have been heard during the Renaissance. How is it different from today's music?

🔍 **Renaissance music viola**

> **"In essence, the Renaissance was simply the green end of one of civilization's hardest winters."**
>
> JOHN FOWLES (1926–2005), TWENTIETH-CENTURY ENGLISH NOVELIST

Other Renaissance inventions simply made everyday life more pleasant or made it possible to complete tasks more quickly. Where would students be if Switzerland's Conrad Gesner had not invented the pencil back in 1565?

British Inventions

Queen Elizabeth I, who ruled England from 1558 to 1603, wanted to make England a major world power, in part through science and technology. She spent lots of money funding research in a variety of fields. These included navigation, mining, and weapons technology.

British inventors were hard at work during the Renaissance, and they all wanted to know William Cecil. Why? He served as lord treasurer and was the man to see if you needed funding for a new invention.

Cecil was keen to give money to inventors working on more reliable weapons to defend Britain. He also supported those involved in developing industries such as salt manufacturing and glassmaking. New engines and machines were just the kind of inventive projects he would have been likely to support.

FEMALE CARTOGRAPHERS

Women were involved in cartography during the Renaissance and even earlier. The late sixteenth and early seventeenth centuries have been described as "the golden age of cartography." Many mapmaking workshops during this time were family-run. Women helped with different aspects of map creation, such as engraving. Others were colorists, whose job it was to add colors to parts of the map, such as political borders and decorative elements. Other women had the task of carefully stitching the leaves of a map into a book. Why do you think more men are remembered for their contributions to cartography than women?

Sixteenth-century cannons. William Cecil was interested in funding inventions such as these to better defend the country against attackers.

credit: Agostino Ramelli

Of course, not all British inventions during this time were focused on warfare or large-scale industry. Some had to do with everyday items. For example, bottled beer was invented in London in 1568. And 35 years later, Francis Bacon invented a way to freeze chicken! Today, both of these are still part of everyday life for people around the globe.

What other Renaissance invention from Britain is essential to peoples' lives around the world? The flush toilet, invented in 1591 by Sir John Harrington!

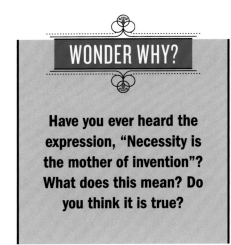

WONDER WHY?

Have you ever heard the expression, "Necessity is the mother of invention"? What does this mean? Do you think it is true?

Drawing of a pendulum clock designed by Galileo Galilei around 1641

Why Did They Invent?

The Renaissance was a productive time for inventors. Why? Was genius in the water? There are many possible reasons why Renaissance inventors designed and created so many amazing new things.

For one thing, the Middle Ages was really a time of economic decline, when many people just scraped by. Gradually, people began moving to cities, where they could earn more money and more of a middle class came into existence. Not everyone had to farm anymore. Some of these people became inventors.

During the Renaissance, people had a new confidence in what they were capable of doing. This led to an explosion of new ideas and information.

Renaissance thinkers and scientists alike wanted to bring their culture back to life. They did this in part by expanding and reinterpreting the ideas from cultures such as ancient Greece and Rome. Renaissance inventors tended to be curious about the world and even the universe.

Some inventors might have hoped to gain fame and fortune through their inventions, but many were simply in pursuit of knowledge. And there's no doubt that today's world is richer because of the creations and discoveries of Renaissance inventors.

CONNECT

Leonardo da Vinci is perhaps the best known figure from the Renaissance. Not only was he an inventor, he was also a painter, sculptor, scientist, and philosopher. Watch a video about his work here. Do you know anyone working today who is similar to Leonardo?

 Leonardo da Vinci videopedia

WORDS OF WONDER

This book is packed with lots of new vocabulary! Try figuring out the meanings of unfamiliar words using the context and roots of the words. There is a glossary in the back to help you and Words of Wonder check-ins for every chapter.

Are You an Inventor?

Being a inventor during the Renaissance was exciting. There were new discoveries to make and new devices to create. At times, it was also dangerous. Some new scientific ideas went against what was generally accepted at the time.

Some scientists, including Galileo Galilei, were harshly punished for sharing their new ideas about the universe. Heliocentrism was one of these ideas. This is the belief that the sun, not the earth, is the center of the solar system. Why do you think some people refused to believe this?

In *The Renaissance Inventors*, you'll meet five famous inventors who showed creativity and innovation while thinking up new ways of doing things. You'll also learn about several other inventors who thrived during the Renaissance, including women and people of color. Let's get started!

Gutenberg in a sixteenth-century copper engraving by Nicolas de Larmessin

CHAPTER 1

JOHANNES
Gutenberg

Gutenberg's design of a printing press, modeled after grape and olive presses

Johannes Gutenberg was a German inventor and craftsman who lived during the fifteenth century. His invention of the printing press allowed culture and information to spread in a way it never could before, through the mass production of books, pamphlets, and other printed materials.

FAST FACTS

BIRTH DATE: C. 1398

PLACE OF BIRTH: MAINZ, GERMANY

AGE AT DEATH: ABOUT 70 (DIED FEBRUARY 3, 1468)

FAMOUS ACCOMPLISHMENT: INVENTOR OF THE PRINTING PRESS

Why was this so important? Remember, before the printing press there was no easy way to print books. People had to rely on other people and the church to get their news and information about the world. Why might this be a problem? How might this give too much power to people who had access to the very few books in the world? Let's take a look at Gutenberg's beginnings.

WONDER WHY?

Can you think of examples of inventors who applied the skills they learned in different industries to their inventions?

HISTORY'S MYSTERIES

For some people who lived long ago, we have plenty of information about when they did certain things. However, for some historical figures, we have very little accurate information. Historians and biographers are constantly striving to fix errors as new records and artifacts are discovered. If someone had to make a timeline of your lifetime 100 years after you died, how would they know they were using the right dates? Why is accuracy important in the study of history?

Early Life

Johannes Gutenberg was born around the year 1398 in the bustling German port city of Mainz, located on the Rhine River. His mother, Else Wirich, was a shopkeeper's daughter. His father, Friele Gensfleisch zur Laden, had been married before and had a daughter named Patze from his first marriage. Gutenberg also had an older brother named Friele and an older sister named Else.

Johannes Gutenberg
c. 1398–1468

c. 1398
Gutenberg is born in Mainz, Germany.

1434
Gutenberg settles in Strasbourg.

c. 1439
Gutenberg improves on different printing designs to create a new kind of printing press.

1448
Gutenberg prints the 1448 calendar, which becomes available to a wide audience for the first time.

The Gutenberg Monument in Mainz

DOROTEA BUCCA

Today, it's very common for women to be doctors and scientists. But back in the fourteenth century, that was definitely not the case! Women were more likely to practice traditional medicine based on herb gathering. One exception was an Italian woman named Dorotea Bucca. Born in 1360, she became a physician. She was one of the first scientists in Europe to help open the field of science to other women.

His father worked in the mint in Mainz. The mint produced several different products for the city, including official coins, medals, and jewelry.

Although he didn't do a formal apprenticeship, it's likely that Gutenberg learned how to melt and form metals by working with his dad or his uncle. Working at the mint, Gutenberg would have learned how to cut precious stones, too.

1450
He begins operating a print shop in Mainz, which he funds by borrowing money from other people.

1455
Gutenberg completes his first Bible using his new printing press.

1455
Johann Fust sues Gutenberg for money owed and wins.

1468
Gutenberg dies in Mainz.

Gutenberg's family was wealthy. He didn't have to work as a child, as many did at the time. Gutenberg first went to school in Mainz, where he further developed his talent for research and discovery. Latin was one of the subjects Gutenberg studied there.

Some historians believe Johannes Gutenberg studied at a German university called Erfurt. After all, many sons of wealthy families in Mainz went to school there to study grammar, logic, philosophy, physics, and astronomy.

Then, during the autumn of 1419, Gutenberg's father died. From what few documents exist, it seems that there was a dispute about the inheritance left to him by his father.

No records tell us exactly what Gutenberg did during the next decade. It's one of the many mysteries of the Renaissance!

> "Every year, especially since 1563, the number of writings published in every field is greater than all those produced in the past thousand years."
>
> **JOHANNES KEPLER (1571–1631), GERMAN THINKER**

RENAISSANCE APPRENTICESHIPS

Today, almost all young people in the United States and other developed countries go to school or are taught at home. But during the Renaissance, that wasn't the case. Boys from wealthy families often attended school, while most girls were not educated. It was common for teens (more males than females) to do apprenticeships to learn trades, including goldsmithing, printing, blacksmithing, and sewing. Apprentices typically lived in the homes of master craftsmen. They learned their craft as an apprentice for seven or even 10 years. The hands-on training left people well prepared for their new jobs. Renaissance apprentices include Leonardo da Vinci!

Gutenberg as Entrepreneur

In the early 1430s, Gutenberg left Mainz and moved to Strasbourg, which was located in modern-day France, about 125 miles away. Strasbourg was a much bigger city with more opportunities.

Sadly, Gutenberg's mother died in 1433. However, he received quite a lot of money after her death, which helped him pursue some of his career goals.

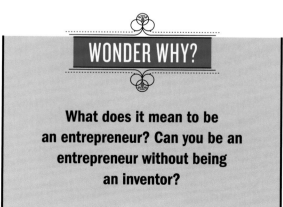

Strasbourg, France, as it looks today.

credit: ChristinaT (CC BY 2.0)

Gutenberg was able to make a living as an inventor in Strasbourg. He created a new technique for polishing gemstones and taught this technique to other people. One of his students was a wealthy man named Andreas Dritzehn.

Gutenberg, Dritzehn, and two other men, Hans Riffe and Andreas Heilmann, formed a manufacturing cooperative. In a cooperative, members of a business or organization own the business together and share its profits.

This cooperative's initial project was making holy mirrors, which were small mirrors they planned to sell to pilgrims traveling to Aachen. The pilgrims believed the mirrors would be able to heal people and animals. Producing holy mirrors for pilgrims shows that Gutenberg was an entrepreneur, as well as an inventor.

> "What the world is today, good and bad, it owes to Gutenberg."
>
> **MARK TWAIN (1835–1910), AMERICAN WRITER**

WONDER WHY?

What does it mean to be an entrepreneur? Can you be an entrepreneur without being an inventor?

Printing and Privacy

While in Strasbourg, Gutenberg also worked as a partner in a printing shop. When he started working there, the printing process was slow and labor intensive. Every single new page required someone to create a brand-new printing form. This was usually a block of wood that was cut with the shapes of the letters.

Gutenberg was interested in finding a way to make metal casts of all the individual letters of the alphabet. With a big enough supply of such letters, a printer could use them over and over—saving lots of time and money!

"After the birth of printing books became widespread. Hence everyone throughout Europe devoted himself to the study of literature. . . . I really believe that at last the world is alive, indeed seething, and that the stimuli of these remarkable conjunctions did not act in vain."

JOHANNES KEPLER

IN THE ISLAMIC WORLD

By the time the Renaissance was taking place in Europe, there were many universities operating throughout the continent that had been founded during the Middle Ages. But where did the knowledge taught in these universities come from? Almost every single text read in the early European university had been translated from Arabic, the language of the Islam. The sciences had flourished in the Islamic world and it was Muslim learning, in the texts written by Muslims for Muslims, that formed the basis of almost every single class at the medieval European university. Al-Qarawiyyin in Fes, Morocco, became an important center of learning in Africa, with many areas of study such as mathematics, chemistry, medicine, and astronomy. Cairo, Egypt, was also an ancient center of learning that contributed much to the Renaissance in Europe.

Gutenberg had many technical challenges to overcome while inventing the printing process. Here are some of them.

+ Creating a metal alloy that would melt at low enough temperatures so it could easily be poured into letter molds

+ Developing an ink that would transfer impressions from metal to paper in a neat, crisp manner

+ Discovering a force that could be used to create these impressions from letter to paper

Gutenberg wanted to work on a better method of printing. He knew that if he could mass-produce books, he might become a rich man. But he didn't want anyone to steal his ideas. So, he began working in secret.

Lawsuits and Secret Projects

When Johannes Gutenberg formed the cooperative to make holy mirrors with his Strasbourg colleagues, these men helped him finance the cooperative's projects. These partners weren't happy when they discovered Gutenberg was working on secret projects! They felt they should be partners in all his activities.

Gutenberg ended up revealing his printing press plans. His partners were very excited and believed they could make lots of money if Gutenberg's printing press really did come to be.

In 1438, Gutenberg signed a five-year contract with Riffe, Dritzehn, and Heilmann. This contract said that if any one of the partners died, the partners' heirs could not join their partnership.

A horrible disease known as the plague struck in 1438, killing Andreas Dritzehn. Dritzehn's heirs took Gutenberg to court, demanding that they be made partners. But they lost the lawsuit.

THE BLACK DEATH

Back in the Renaissance, doctors didn't have the ability to fight off infectious diseases. One of the most scary diseases of this time was the Black Death. This plague spread like wildfire through the unsanitary towns and cities of Europe between 1348 and 1350. People caught it from being bitten by infected rat fleas. This terrible epidemic was called the Black Death because black buboes, or swellings, would appear in the victim's armpits or groin. If a bubo burst on its own, the victim might survive. But many didn't. In fact, it's estimated that 30 to 60 percent of Europe's population died from this grim disease.

A plague doctor, who visited those infected by the plague during epidemics

By Paulus Fürst Excud, circa 1656

WONDER WHY?

Do you think it was fair that Gutenberg's partners demanded to see his projects? Why or why not?

Movable Type

Johannes Gutenberg plugged away at the design of his printing press. He also worked on making metal type, which are sets of letters made from metal. He experimented with many, perhaps even hundreds of combinations of metals before he came up with an alloy that worked well for the type.

Why was this so tricky? The metal needed to have two important qualities. It had to have a low enough melting point to be cast into type easily, but also be hard enough to last through many uses.

During the casting process, Gutenberg poured molten metal into a mold to give it a shape. In the end, Gutenberg decided on an alloy that was 80-percent lead, 15-percent antimony, and 5-percent tin.

Metal movable type was a huge innovation given to Europe by Gutenberg. Up to that point, European printers had to carve a solid block of wood to make a single page.

Letterpress set up for printing. Imagine if this was how you had to print out your homework every night!

"It is a press, certainly, but a press from which shall flow in inexhaustible streams . . . . Through it, God will spread His Word. A spring of truth shall flow from it: like a new star it shall scatter the darkness of ignorance, and cause a light heretofore unknown to shine amongst men."

JOHANNES GUTENBERG

Thanks to Gutenberg's new system, printers could reuse the type by simply rearranging the letters to print new pages. Gutenberg cast almost 300 different shapes of type. These included upper and lowercase letters, punctuation marks, and symbols.

By 1448, Gutenberg had returned to Mainz. He had worked out enough of the kinks in the printing process to convince a man named Johann Fust (c. 1400–1466) to invest money in his new printing shop.

Gutenberg worked mostly behind closed doors for the next few years, perfecting his amazing invention. Several scholars believe that during the 1440s, Gutenberg started to experiment with printing individual sheets of paper and perhaps even small books.

TILL DEATH DO US . . .

In 1437, a woman named Ennlein zur Yserin Thüre took Gutenberg to court, claiming he'd promised to marry her. Gutenberg denied the claim, but had to pay a fee to her family. Johannes never married Ennlein. Historians don't know if he ever married!

How Did It Work?

Gutenberg invented three things that led to his worldwide success. One was sturdy movable type. Movable type had been invented in China centuries earlier, but it was very fragile and never caught on in Europe. Another was the actual printing press. And the third was ink that would stick well to the type rather than run off, as many water-based inks tended to do.

Gutenberg's invention was a combination of several different technologies. His press used block printing, which was a Chinese technique Marco Polo brought back to Europe. Gutenberg combined it with the type of press that was used to make olive oil and wine.

A printing press in use
By Jost Amman, 1568

SMALL ART

So, what was the first book Gutenberg published? Scholars believe it was probably a Latin grammar textbook called *Ars Minor*, or *The Smaller Art*. It is believed that there are existing copies of *Ars Minor* that date back to 1451, even before Gutenberg's famous Bible.

You can see the text of *Ars Minor* at this website. It's in Latin! Do you recognize any words or parts of words?

🔍 **Ars Minor intratext**

Gutenberg would likely have been familiar with such a press, since he grew up in a region of Germany that made wine. The type of press Gutenberg used could apply pressure evenly to a piece of paper or vellum laid on top of the metal type. The paper was often slightly damp.

Here's how Gutenberg's printing press worked, step by step.

✦ People arrange the movable type onto a flat wooden plate known as the lower platen.

✦ They apply ink to the metal type, which are the letter forms.

✦ They place a sheet of paper on top of the inked type.

✦ They lower the upper platen until it meets the lower platen. At this point, the two plates push together the paper and type to create clear, sharp images on the paper.

Voilà—a printed page!

WONDER WHY?

Can you think of other inventions that have helped spread knowledge as much as Gutenberg's printing press? If so, which ones?

The beginning of the Gutenberg Bible, Volume 1, Old Testament, Epistle of St. Jerome

Books and More Books

Around 1455, Johannes Gutenberg completed his first printing of the Bible. The Gutenberg Bible is also sometimes referred to as the 42-line Bible because every page had 42 lines in each column of its double-column pages. A person known as an illuminator added the finishing touches to each Bible, such as red and blue headers, initials, and text.

Only three perfect vellum copies of the Gutenberg Bible are known to exist. One is in the U.S. Library of Congress in Washington, DC. The others are at the British Library in London, England and the Bibliothèque Nationale in Paris, France.

People were very impressed with the quality of those first copies. But these Bibles weren't cheap—they cost the equivalent of several years' salaries for an average male worker of the time!

CONNECT

You can look at the Gutenberg Bible on the Library of Congress website. You can view many different pages from the book.

Library of Congress Gutenberg Bible

How could regular people buy books? As the printing process continued to improve, books got cheaper.

You might think Gutenberg got rich right away from coming up with such a genius idea as the printing press. But he'd borrowed lots of money to work on the project before it was perfected. This turned out to be a problem.

In 1455, Gutenberg's business partner, Johann Fust, sued Gutenberg for the money Fust had lent him. Gutenberg didn't have the money to repay what Fust had loaned him!

WONDER WHY?

Why do you think Gutenberg had so much trouble with lawsuits? Do you think he should have done anything differently to avoid his legal problems?

Sadly, Gutenberg lost the lawsuit. He had to turn over his Bible workshop to Fust and possibly even some of the Bibles that had already been printed.

Even though he had lost his workshop, he was able to print some other works, possibly using other printing workshops in Mainz or nearby Eltville.

While you might picture the man who invented the printing press as working with his device into old age, very little is known about Gutenberg's last years. Some historians believe he went blind before he died in the town where he was born on February 3, 1468.

EARLY PRINTING IN CHINA

There is no doubt that Gutenberg revolutionized the world of printing. But he wasn't the first person to create printed documents. The history of printing dates back hundreds of years before Gutenberg! Almost 600 years before his time, monks in China were using a technique called block printing. In this method, carved wooden blocks were coated in ink and then sheets of paper were pressed on top.

The British Library in London has a copy of the oldest surviving complete printed book with a date on it—The *Diamond Sutra*, printed in 868. This book was written in Chinese and is considered a sacred work for Buddhists. In the centuries that followed, woodblock printing continued to advance in China.

> **"I owe all my knowledge to the German inventor, Johannes Gutenberg!"**
>
> **MEHMET MURAT ÎLDAN (1965–), TURKISH PLAYWRIGHT AND NOVELIST**

The Printing Press by John White Alexander, circa 1896

This portion of a mural in the Library of Congress shows someone working an early printing press while Gutenberg and another man examine the print. From the cycle *The Evolution of the Book.* Library of Congress (Jefferson Building), Washington, DC

Legacy

Gutenberg's printing press is one of the most important inventions in history. This amazing device allowed people to produce books and other texts faster, more accurately, and more cheaply than ever before, and in greater numbers.

Before Gutenberg's printing press, mainly the upper classes owned books. But as books became less expensive and more easily available, many more people could get access to them, too. This led to a dramatic increase in the general public's education and literacy.

Today, more words are printed every second than were printed each year in the fifteenth and sixteenth centuries!

Gutenberg's invention brought learning, imagination, and communication to the world. Can you think of inventions from today that have accomplished the same things? What would your life be like if he had never invented the printing press?

WORDS OF WONDER

What vocabulary words did you discover? Can you figure out the meanings of these words by using the context and roots? Look in the glossary for help!

alloy · block printing · cooperative
movable type · plague · vellum

Try Styrofoam Printing

Johannes Gutenberg invented the printing press during the Renaissance. Before this invention, books were made by hand. The text was copied word by word. The printing press made the creation and distribution of books much easier, so more people could have access to books. In this activity, you'll try your own method of printing.

➤ **Cut a Styrofoam sheet into a small square or circle shape, perhaps about 4 to 5 inches in size—it doesn't need to be perfect!**

➤ **Using a pencil, draw a design into the cut piece of Styrofoam.** You'll want to press down hard, but don't rip through it.

➤ **Cover the surface where you are working with newspaper.** Pour some ink onto a plate or into an aluminum paint tray.

➤ **Roll a mini paint roller lightly though the ink.** Then roll the inked roller over your Styrofoam design.

➤ **Place the inked Styrofoam onto a piece of paper.** Make sure to push down lightly so that the whole design is pressed into the paper.

➤ **Remove the Styrofoam and admire your new print work.** Can you think of ways to make your printing go faster? How can you be neater? Are there other ways you can improve the process?

WONDER WHY?

Do you find that you have less time to be creative when there is a lot of hard work to do? In your experience, does hard work ever fuel creativity?

Stamp Your Message

Making multiple copies of a hand-printed document can take time. How fast can you get your message out?

> ➤ **Come up with a very short message using sets of rubber alphabet stamps.** This could be just a sentence or two.

> ➤ **Glue the rubber stamps to a piece of wood.** The letter side should be facing you and the flat side should be glued down. Allow the glue to dry completely before using.

> ➤ **Using an inkpad or ink roller, lightly coat all the stamps in a layer of ink.**

> ➤ **Holding the edges of the wood piece, place the inked stamps face down onto a piece of paper, starting at the top of the page.** Re-ink the stamps and press the stamps down onto the paper, just below the first line you did.

> ➤ **Repeat until you have filled the page with text.**

> ➤ **Can you make multiple sheets with the same text?** How long does it take?

BI SHENG

While Johannes Gutenberg often gets the credit for inventing movable type, that's not entirely accurate. Many centuries before, people in other nations created such type. A Chinese inventor named Bi Sheng (990–1051) is said to have invented movable type made of a mixture of clay and a type of glue in the eleventh century. This type had to be baked to harden. Unfortunately, it was quite fragile. Scholars have also found wooden movable type dating back to the late twelfth and early thirteenth centuries in China. And both wooden and metal movable type appeared in Korea during the fourteenth century.

A statue of Leon Battista Alberti in Florence, Italy

CHAPTER 2

LEON BATTISTA
Alberti

A portrait of Alberti by G. Benaglia, eighteenth century

Sometimes, inventors create new products. They can also create new ways for people to see and think about things. Inventors can change the perspective of a whole community by bringing new ideas to light.

Leon Battista Alberti was this kind of inventor.

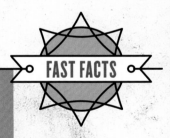

FAST FACTS

BIRTH DATE:
FEBRUARY 14, 1404
PLACE OF BIRTH:
GENOA, ITALY
AGE AT DEATH: 68 (DIED APRIL 25, 1472)
FAMOUS ACCOMPLISHMENT: HE WROTE DETAILED BOOKS ON ART AND ARCHITECTURE, AS WELL AS PHILOSOPHY.

A fifteenth-century Italian writer, architect, and inventor, Leon Battista Alberti wrote works of philosophy in Italian rather than Latin. This made them accessible to more people. His book on classical architecture was considered an essential tool for architects. Alberti's inventions spanned fields from art to science.

Alberti's Early Years

Leon Battista Alberti was born in 1404 in the Italian port city of Genoa. Alberti's father, Lorenzo Alberti, was a merchant from Florence. His mother was a widow from Bologna. He had an older brother named Carlo. Alberti's parents weren't married when he was born.

A portrait of Alberti from 1568

WONDER WHY?

Why might someone born to unmarried parents be treated badly? Does this happen today? Can you think of any other family structures that are discriminated against today?

Back in the early 1400s, children born to unmarried parents were sometimes treated badly by their families. Luckily, Alberti's father treated him very well. However, even as a young boy, Alberti felt the need to defend his reputation.

Not much is known about whether Alberti had a relationship with his mother, but he did have a stepmother.

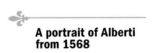

Leon Battista Alberti
1404–1472

1404
Alberti is born in Genoa, Italy.

1416–18
Alberti attends Gasparino da Barzizza's prestigious boarding school in Padua.

1428
Alberti receives his doctorate in canon law from the University of Bologna.

1435
Alberti writes the book *On Painting*.

When he was a young boy, Alberti's family moved to Venice, Italy. By 1414, his father managed the Venetian branch of the Alberti family's successful trading company. This business had offices as far away as England, France, the Greek islands, and beyond. What did this mean for young Alberti? For one thing, his family was rich.

Education

Alberti's dad provided him with an excellent education. His father gave him early training in math, sparking a lifelong fondness of the subject. Alberti delighted in its practical uses. He also liked how ordered and rational math was. Later in life, Alberti used math to help figure out the principles used in painting, such as perspective. He also used math in his scientific experiments.

CONNECT

Take a look at one of Alberti's famous architectural designs!

🔍 **Palazzo Rucellai Khan**

CATHERINE DE MEDICI

Not everyone interested in architecture during the Renaissance was male. Catherine de Medici was born in Italy but became a French queen in the sixteenth century. She was involved in the construction of a number of architectural gems in France. These included a new wing of the famous Louvre Museum, the Tuileries Gardens, and the château of Monceau, near Paris. Writer Paul Van Dyke said of her, "It seems certain that in architecture at least Catherine had her own taste and possessed some skill."

From about 1416 to 1418, Alberti attended the famous school run by Gasparino da Barzizza (1360–1431). This boarding school was in the city of Padua, about 24 miles west of Venice. Today, you can whip down the highway between these two cities in about 45 minutes. But that wasn't the case in Alberti's day! He probably didn't go home that often.

1450
Alberti invents the first mechanical anemometer.

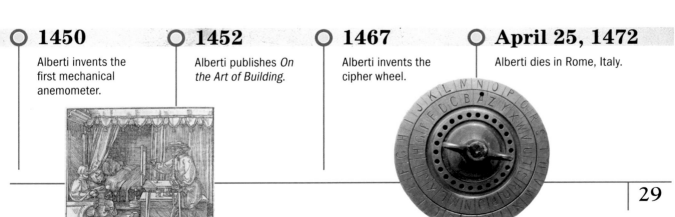

1452
Alberti publishes *On the Art of Building.*

1467
Alberti invents the cipher wheel.

April 25, 1472
Alberti dies in Rome, Italy.

At school, Alberti studied the Latin classics and perhaps some Greek ones, too. The Renaissance concept of humanism was an important part of the curriculum. Students studied the works of ancient Greek and Latin authors. Moral philosophy, the study of right and wrong, was another focus of the school.

Alberti was full of ambition. After Barzizza's school, he attended the University of Bologna, where he studied law. His future looked bright. Unfortunately, after his first year as a university student, tragedy struck. In March 1421, Alberti's father died.

WONDER WHY?

Why do people who are feeling stress sometimes get physically sick? Has that ever happened to you? How do you handle stress?

WHOSE PLAY IS IT?

When Alberti was 20 years old and a student at the University of Bologna, he wrote a Latin comedy titled *Philodoxus*. But Alberti did not reveal himself as the author of this work. Instead, he used the pen name "Lepidus." Why did he do this? No one can say for certain. Perhaps he worried that no one would believe such a young writer had created the comedy. Or maybe he had a wicked sense of humor. Regardless of the reason, for 10 years, many people believed that *Philodoxus* was the work of a Roman named Lepidus. Eventually, Alberti wanted to present this work as his own. But not everyone believed him. In 1588, a scholarly press published the comedy—not as the work of Alberti, but as that of Lepidus.

This was a blow to Alberti, who depended on his dad for financial support. Not long after his father's death, Alberti's own health took a turn for the worse as the pressure of serious studies wore on him.

Did Alberti give up? No. Instead, he changed his focus. He began studying both the visual arts and nature. These new passions occupied his attention for the rest of his life. Alberti also started writing some of his own pieces of literature in Latin. His writing began slowly, but he kept plugging away.

CONNECT

Take a look at an architectural plan for a bridge, which Alberti helped design.

🔍 **LOC Alberti architectural**

Alberti studied at Bologna for seven years and received a doctorate in canon law in 1428. Canon law is a special branch of law that deals with the Catholic Church, especially the study of laws made by the pope.

From Friendship to Flops

In 1428, Alberti went to Florence. This city was an amazing place to be at the time. It was a center of culture. The visual arts being created here were incredible.

Science and technology were also thriving in Florence. Huge advances were being made in medicine, math, architecture, and engineering. In Florence, Alberti met Filippo Brunelleschi (1377–1446), a pioneer in Italian Renaissance architecture. They were both interested in math and the two became friends. It was through Brunelleschi that Alberti grew interested in architecture.

In the 1430s, Alberti took a job in Rome, Italy. He worked as a secretary in the administrative offices for the pope. He was paid to rewrite the lives of martyrs and saints in classical Latin. For the rest of his days, he earned a living from the Church. This gave him financial stability and independence.

An image of Filippo Brunelleschi, from Masaccio's painting *Raising of the Son of Theophilus and St. Peter Enthroned*, in the Brancacci Chapel, Florence

FILIPPO BRUNELLESCHI

Filippo Brunelleschi was a good friend and a mentor to Alberti. But he was also a very important Renaissance figure on his own. Born in Florence in 1477, he trained both as a goldsmith and a sculptor. One of his best-known sculptures is *The Sacrifice of Isaac*. Brunelleschi turned to architecture later in his career. While he didn't design many buildings, he is especially famous for his work on the cathedral in Florence. Its impressive dome was an engineering feat many considered impossible. Brunelleschi was an excellent example of the motto "Hard work pays off." Even though he had no formal training as an engineer or architect, he brought new ideas to all the buildings he touched.

During his early days working for the Church, Alberti started to write in Italian, as well as Latin. Remember, Latin was the language of scholars and well-educated people at the time—so why would Alberti also write in Italian? This was a way to reach more people. Alberti wrote works of philosophy geared toward the common person. These provided words of wisdom on many subjects, from family and friendship to education and dealing with misfortune.

WONDER WHY?

Why is it important for writers to reach as wide an audience as possible? Why might some people have wanted to limit the number of people able to read books?

> "He enjoyed literature so much that it sometimes gave him the same pleasure as the buds of sweetly smelling flowers, and then neither hunger nor sleep could make him leave his books."
>
> **ANONYMOUS**

In the mid-1430s, Alberti moved back to Florence along with Pope Eugenius IV (1383–1447), who'd been driven out of Rome after people revolted against him. From 1435 to 1452, Alberti expressed his creativity in many ways.

CONNECT

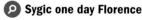

Take a photo tour of Florence!

🔍 **Sygic one day Florence**

He wrote about the lives of Florentine clans and the practices of Florentine painters. He worked hard to become one of Italy's top experts in ancient architecture and art.

Did Alberti ever experience failure? You bet! Once, Alberti organized a public poetry contest, but it turned out to be a massive flop. No one was interested! Perhaps not everyone in Florence was as intellectual as Alberti might have hoped. But that didn't stop him from trying new things.

Art and Invention

Alberti was always looking to expand his mind. When his artistic friends struggled with practical or technical problems related to their work, Alberti was keen to help them figure things out.

One of Alberti's great successes as a writer had to do with art. In 1435, he wrote a book titled *On Painting.* The book clearly explained how to draw a picture that showed a three-dimensional scene on the two-dimensional surface. This book was an incredibly useful tool for artists. It had a huge influence on Italian relief work and paintings. In addition, it helped to bring forth the new Renaissance style using perspective.

How do you draw a three-dimensional scene on a flat surface? All you need is paper, a ruler, and a pencil.

Start by drawing a horizontal line across the middle of your paper—this is the horizon. Choose a point on that line to be your vanishing point. This is the spot you'll think of as being farthest away from you, the point at which objects are so small they disappear.

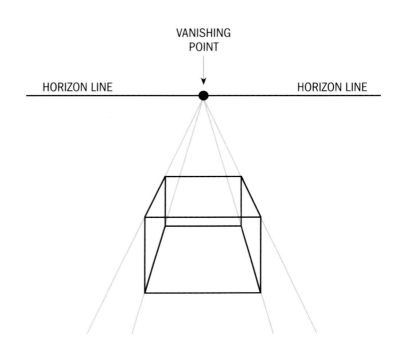

VANISHING POINT

HORIZON LINE   HORIZON LINE

Use your ruler to lightly sketch lines that go from the vanishing point to the edge of the paper. With these guides in place, you can draw objects on the paper that look three-dimensional. Start with simpler drawings of different shapes. Everything above the horizon will appear as though you're looking at it from underneath. Everything below the line will appear as though you're looking down from above it.

Once you've gotten the hang of drawing from one perspective, you can draw an entire room or cityscape using the same method.

Alberti the Architect

Do you ever look at a building and wonder how it got the way it is?

Alberti was fascinated with architecture and engineering. He read as much as he could from classical texts about ancient statues and buildings. He was a very thorough researcher, but he also believed in hands-on research. As biographer Anthony Grafton wrote, Alberti turned "over the rubble of every site he could reach." By 1447, when Nicholas V (1397–1455) became the new pope, Alberti had gained enough engineering knowledge to become the pope's architectural advisor.

> **"So great was his genius that he may be said to have been master of all the arts."**
>
> **ANONYMOUS**

In 1452, Alberti published a mega-work on architecture. It was called *De re aedificatoria,* or *On the Art of Building.* It consisted of 10 chapters in about 400 pages. Some have called this work "a bible for Renaissance architecture." This book was essential to peoples' understanding of architecture in the fifteenth century.

On the Art of Building celebrated and advanced the knowledge of engineering from ancient times. Specifically, Alberti addressed concerns about proportion in architecture. He provided practical advice to builders and architects of his own day.

Architecture was a central focus for Alberti during the 1450s and 1460s. But he didn't just write about the nuts and bolts of architectural or engineering practices. He also designed some incredible buildings during the last 20 years of his life.

Some writers have said Alberti applied mathematical principles to achieve perfect proportion in his architectural designs.

Alberti designed or helped to design several famous buildings in Italy. One is a church called Santa Maria Novella, located in Florence. Its beautiful marble façade continues to thrill visitors to this day.

Alberti also designed the façade of another famous building in Florence: the Palazzo Rucellai. This was the home of a rich merchant family. Alberti put serious thought into every element of this home's front, from its flattened columns to the round arches of the windows. Today, scholars feel the façade of this building stands apart from any other of the medieval period.

Santa Maria Novella, with a marble facade, located in Florence

Palazzo Rucellai, designed by Alberti
credit: Miguel Hermoso Cuesta

More Incredible Inventions

Alberti's drive and intellectual curiosity seemed to have no end. In 1450, he invented the world's first mechanical anemometer. This is a device that measures wind speed.

Alberti's anemometer was made of a disk placed perpendicular to whatever direction the wind was blowing. The wind would make the disk spin. By looking at the angle of inclination of the disk, you could tell how much force the wind had. If the wind was stronger, the disk would be at a greater angle. If the wind wasn't so strong, the disk wouldn't be inclined much.

Have you ever wanted to send a secret message to someone? Alberti worked for years for the pope's office, where it might have been important to keep things secret. Maybe this is what led him to create another super-cool invention in 1467: the cipher wheel.

This handy tool helped create and decode secret messages. The cipher wheel is considered a pioneering work in the field of cryptography. Here's how it worked.

Alberti's cipher wheel consisted of two disks. The outer disk didn't move, while the inner disk rotated. On the outer disk were the uppercase letters of the Latin alphabet. The Latin alphabet is the same as the English alphabet, minus J, U, and W.

WONDER WHY?

Can you think of other ways of measuring the force of wind? How do scientists measure wind speed today?

An example of a cipher wheel

Alberti also left out H, K, and Y, since he thought they were unnecessary. The outer disk also included numbers 1 through 4. The inner disk included the lowercase alphabet (without u, w, and j), but in a random order. It also had the word *et*, meaning "and" in Latin. Alberti's cipher wheel is known as a polyalphabetic cipher, meaning it uses more than one alphabet.

To encrypt or decode a message, the user needed to mark off which spot on the inner disk had been lined up with which spot on the outer disk.

Leon Battista Alberti continued to pursue knowledge, travel, write, and create until his death in Rome in 1472. His ideas and inventions continue to influence writers, artists, and architects even today.

The Topkapi Palace in Turkey

THE TOPKAPI PALACE

While it's true that architects such as Alberti created incredible structures in Italy, skilled architects around the globe were also creating amazing buildings outside of Renaissance Europe. One architectural masterpiece was the Topkapi Palace located in Istanbul, Turkey. This building housed the Ottoman Empire's court. Construction on this building began in the 1450s, at the command of Mehmet the Conqueror. Some say that Mehmet designed the palace himself, though he employed many architects to work on the project. From ceremonial gates to vast courtyards to gardens featuring geometrical designs of vegetable and fruit beds, the Topkapi Palace was stunning. Domes were used in many different spaces of the palace. Colorful ceramic tiles and Islamic calligraphy added to the beauty of the structure.

WONDER WHY?

What personal qualities do you think made Leon Battista Alberti successful in so many different fields?

What Makes Him Different?

Leon Battista Alberti was different from other Renaissance inventors in several ways. To begin with, he studied law at the university, rather than science or mathematics. He also spent much of his early career working as a writer.

While some Renaissance inventors focused on specific topics such as physics or astronomy, Alberti was a true Renaissance man. He designed buildings, invented scientific instruments such as the anemometer, and created a new device to help artists better understand perspective. Alberti was also important in that he chose to write in Italian—not just Latin—to share his philosophical ideas with common folks as well as scholars.

WORDS OF WONDER

What vocabulary words did you discover? Can you figure out the meanings of these words by using the context and roots? Look in the glossary for help!

anemometer · cipher · engineering
façade · perspective · show box

Lasting Legacy

Leon Battista Alberti was a key player in the architectural achievements of the Renaissance. Not only did he further peoples' understanding of ancient architecture, but he also contributed both to the solving of architectural challenges and the creation of beautiful new buildings all over Italy.

Alberti's books *On Painting* and *On the Art of Building* still serve as resources to artists, architects, and engineers—centuries after his death.

Basilica di Sant'Andrea in Mantua, designed by Alberti

Detail of the façade of Santa Maria Novella in Florence
credit: Amada44 (CC BY 3.0)

WONDER WHY?

Why do you think Alberti invented so many kinds of things? How did these inventions connect with his written works, if at all?

Make a Cipher Wheel

Create your own secret messages with this cool, easy-to-make cipher wheel.

> ➤ **Trace the template for the cipher wheel.** Use scissors to cut out the two wheels. Glue each of the wheels onto cardstock, then cut these out as well.

> ➤ **Write all 26 letters of the alphabet (one in each box) in the outer boxes of the large wheel.** Repeat this step in the outer boxes of the small wheel.

> ➤ **Punch holes in the centers of both wheels.** You can use a sharp pencil or even a nail, but be careful not to poke yourself. Push a paper fastener first through the small wheel, then through the bigger wheel, and fasten the two wheels together.

> ➤ **To use your wheel, start by matching up the two As.** Then you can decide how many spaces you want to rotate the top wheel. For example, if you rotate the top wheel three spaces to the right, the A on the top wheel will correspond to D on the bottom one. So A=D, B=E, C=F, and so on. Create a message in code, then have a friend decode it. What information will your friend need to know in order to decode your message?

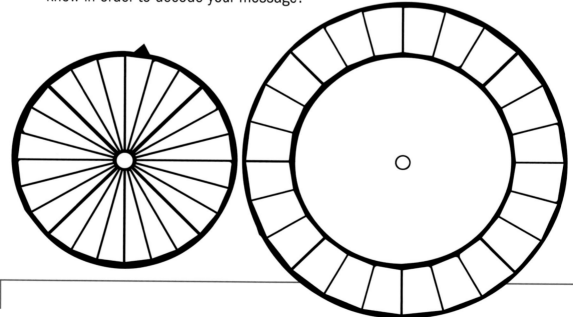

What You Need

five 3-ounce paper cups,
2 straws, pushpin, pencil

Build an Anemometer

Interested in the weather? Check the wind speed with a handmade anemometer.

> **Use a hole punch to punch four holes in one paper cup.** The holes should be just under the rim and evenly spaced.

> **Stick one straw through two holes opposite each other in the cup you just punched.** Place the other straw through the second pair of holes. With a sharp pencil, poke a hole in the center of the bottom of the cup.

> **On another cup, use your hole punch to make two holes about 1 inch apart, about halfway between the bottom and rim of the cup.** Push the end of one of your straws through these two holes. Repeat this step with the three remaining cups. Be sure to face all the cups in the same direction.

> **With its eraser end first, push the pencil into the hole at the bottom of the first cup.** Gently press your pushpin through both straws and into the top of the eraser. Don't jam the pushpin too far into the eraser or the anemometer won't spin. Use your marker to make a circle or line on the side of one of the cups. Why do you think you need this line?

> **Place your anemometer into the wind or near a fan.** Does it spin? How can you improve your design? How can you use the anemometer to measure the speed of the wind?

Leonardo da Vinci

Portrait of Leonardo da Vinci

from Characaturas by Leonardo da Vinci, from *Drawings by Wincelslaus Hollar*

CHAPTER 3

LEONARDO
da Vinci

The Vitruvian Man by Leonardo da Vinci is a study of the proportions of the human body. It was drawn around 1490.

One name from the Renaissance you are sure to recognize is Leonardo da Vinci. He is considered by many to be the epitome of artistry, inventiveness, curiosity, and genius.

FAST FACTS

BIRTH DATE: APRIL 15, 1452

PLACE OF BIRTH: ANCHIANO (NEAR VINCI), REPUBLIC OF FLORENCE, ITALY

AGE AT DEATH: 67 (DIED MAY 2, 1519)

FAMOUS ACCOMPLISHMENT: TOO MANY TO MENTION!

Leonardo da Vinci has been described by some as the most famous artist in the world. But this true Renaissance man was also a brilliant scientist and inventor. During the fifteenth and sixteenth centuries, Leonardo conducted many scientific experiments and invented lots of different devices, including the helicopter and parachute.

> "The human foot is a masterpiece of engineering and a work of art."
>
> **LEONARDO DA VINCI**

Monument to Leonardo da Vinci in the Piazza della Scala in Milan, Italy

Leonardo's Childhood

Leonardo da Vinci was born on April 15, 1452, just outside the Italian city of Florence, in a village called Vinci. Leonardo's mother, Caterina Lippi, was a peasant girl from the Vinci area. His father, Ser Piero, was a notary in Florence. Notaries draw up contracts, deeds, or other important documents.

Can you imagine what it was like in Vinci? The village was built on a hillside, above the plain of the Arno River. Vineyards and olive groves lay below the village, while oak and chestnut trees grew above it.

Leonardo's parents were not married when he was born. At first, he lived with his mother. But within a few years, Leonardo's father took custody of the young boy.

Leonardo da Vinci
1452–1519

1452
Leonardo da Vinci is born in Anchiano, Italy.

c. 1466
Leonardo moves to Florence to become an apprentice at Andrea del Verrocchio's workshop.

1472
Leonardo is accepted into the Florence painters' guild.

1482
Leonardo begins working for Ludovico Sforza, the Duke of Milan.

By the time Leonardo was five years old, he was living with his paternal grandparents. Leonardo might have grown up lonely, were it not for his young and kind uncle Francesco. Francesco farmed his family's land, and Leonardo helped his uncle do farm chores. The two spent time walking and enjoying the countryside. Many sources say that it was Francesco who fostered Leonardo's love of and fascination with nature.

Leonardo received what some people call "a country education." He learned basic arithmetic, writing, and reading.

> **"Learning never exhausts the mind."**
>
> **LEONARDO DA VINCI**

He might have been taught by the local parish priest, or perhaps his grandparents hired a private teacher. Historians aren't sure. We do know that Leonardo didn't study Latin seriously as a boy. He didn't really work hard on higher math, such as advanced geometry, until he was 30.

WONDER WHY?

Do you think Leonardo da Vinci's life would have been any different if he had grown up in a city and gone to university? If so, how and why?

WHAT'S IN A NAME?

Usually, writers use the last names of their subjects when writing biographies. However, Leonardo da Vinci's last name simply means "from Vinci," and using that as an identifier isn't very specific. Plus, Leonardo is such a famous figure that he is most often referred to by just one name: Leonardo.

1496
Leonardo meets the mathematician Luca Pacioli in Milan.

1502–03
Leonardo travels and surveys the lands of Cesare Borgia.

c. 1503
Leonardo starts work on the *Mona Lisa*.

1513
Leonardo moves to Rome to work for Giuliano de' Medici. He continues his studies of botany and anatomy, among other subjects.

1519
Leonardo dies in France on May 2, 1519.

Leonardo Leaves Home

When Leonardo was about 14 years old, he moved to Florence to become an apprentice to an artist named Andrea del Verrocchio (1435–1488).

Most sons of well-to-do parents would have gone to university and studied subjects such as geometry and Latin. But this wasn't an option for Leonardo, because his parents weren't married at the time he was born. Children of unmarried parents couldn't be bankers, doctors, or notaries either. Do you think this was fair?

GUILDS

Guilds were organizations of people with related interests or goals. Merchant guilds were associations of merchants in a town. Craft guilds were associations of artisans and craftspeople such as weavers, architects, painters, and metalsmiths. Guilds were designed to help maintain standards of quality and keep prices stable. Guilds sometimes controlled all the manufacturing and trade in their towns (they were "monopolies"), and there was strict control over who would be accepted into the guild. It wasn't easy to get in!

Since Leonardo had limited career options as a teen, his dad used his connections to help his son. Andrea del Verrocchio was a famous painter and sculptor in Florence. He was an excellent teacher as well.

During his apprenticeship, Leonardo lived with other young men serving as apprentices. Their housing and food were provided as part of the deal. The master also paid his apprentices wages, which increased as their skills improved. Leonardo probably first spent some time doing chores such as sweeping floors and running errands. Later, he would have made brushes, ground pigments to make paints, and prepared panels for painting.

Being an apprentice involved more than boring tasks. At Verrocchio's workshop, Leonardo learned sculpture, painting, and technical arts. He painted altarpieces. He made big sculptures of bronze or marble. He studied and sketched machines and their component parts at Verrocchio's workshop to gain practical knowledge about how they worked. Leonardo also enjoyed chatting about scientific matters with people who visited Verrocchio's workshop.

Verrocchio's famous equine statue, 1488. Leonardo might have helped design and execute this bronze sculpture.

credit: Internet Archive Book Images

In 1472, Leonardo was accepted into Florence's painters' guild. Yet he chose to stay for another five years at Verrocchio's workshop. During this time, he worked on the bronze casting process used for sculpture, among other projects.

Even after leaving Andrea del Verrocchio's workshop around 1477, it is suspected that Leonardo offered to help his former master when Verrocchio received a commission to make a huge equestrian monument. Leonardo might have created sketches, studied the anatomy of horses, and helped Verrocchio's team.

WONDER WHY?

Why did studying equine anatomy help Leonardo create equine sculptures?

"The natural desire of good men is knowledge."

LEONARDO DA VINCI

WAS LEONARDO GAY?

According to many historical accounts, Leonardo da Vinci was very good-looking and charming. He dressed well and socialized with men and women of the highest classes of society, including royalty. Yet, despite all his charms, Leonardo was never known to be in a romantic relationship with a woman. Was Leonardo da Vinci too busy to have a wife? Maybe, but probably not. Throughout the centuries, many scholars have suggested that Leonardo was gay. In 1476, he was summoned to the Office of the Night in Florence, along with three male companions. He was accused of having had homosexual encounters. Back in the fifteenth century, this was a crime. Leonardo claimed innocence, and eventually, the charges were dismissed. Without a time machine, it's unlikely anyone will ever be sure if Leonardo was gay.

A drawing of a siege machine by Leonardo, circa 1480

New Challenges

By 1481, Leonardo was ready to move on from Florence. He wanted to try new things, see new places. Luckily, Leonardo had made connections with some of Florence's elite, including Lorenzo de' Medici (1449–1488). Lorenzo was rich, powerful, and supportive of Leonardo.

Lorenzo de' Medici helped Leonardo get a job working for a friend of his, the duke of Milan—also known as Ludovico Sforza (1452–1508). But Leonardo didn't get the job immediately. He wrote a letter to the duke explaining his skills. Leonardo knew the duke had an appetite for war, so he told the duke of his skills as a military engineer.

He said he'd studied the latest and greatest war machines and had suggestions for improvements as well as ideas for new machines. From portable bridges to covered vehicles, Leonardo promised his new boss a wide variety of innovations that could help Milan in the event of conflict.

Leonardo also mentioned that he was highly skilled in architecture, could build sculptures and bridges, and was a terrific painter.

Was Leonardo making promises he couldn't keep? Not necessarily. While in Florence, Leonardo created many technical sketches of items ranging from military weapons and pumps to mechanical apparatuses.

WONDER WHY?

Accounts show that Leonardo had a healthy ego and wasn't afraid to show off his skills. Do you think he would have been as successful and famous if he'd been more modest and shy?

Renaissance craftsman and artists often could both build and repair common types of machines. But inventing new ones was unusual. Leonardo was unique in his attitude toward machines. He figured that if he knew how all the different parts of a machine functioned, he could adapt and combine them in new ways to either improve upon machines that already existed or to create brand new ones.

Life in Milan

Leonardo started working for the duke of Milan in 1482. He stayed in Milan for 17 years, until Ludovico Sforza fell from power.

Leonardo was busy during this time. He was often consulted as an architectural or military advisor. Sometimes, he'd paint or make sculptures. He also designed sets for special events or court festivals.

Leonardo da Vinci created some of his most famous works of art during this time in Milan, including an altar painting titled *The Virgin of the Rocks* and his mural painting *The Last Supper.*

These paintings helped establish Leonardo even further as an artistic genius.

The Virgin of the Rocks, 1485

Oil on a wood panel, 48 inches by 78 inches

Around 1485, Leonardo came up with detailed plans for an ornithopter, a human-powered, wing-flapping device. However, there isn't evidence that he tried to build one. He also designed a "helical airscrew," which looks like a modern-day helicopter. It was one of his many unsuccessful inventions. Why didn't the helical airscrew work? It didn't have a source of power strong enough to give it propulsion and lift. It was an idea ahead of its time.

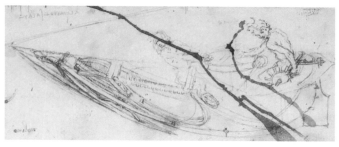

Leonardo came up with many ideas that were ahead of their time. Visions of the submarine, airplane, and the car appeared in his drawings. Even 500 years after he drew them, lots of Leonardo's sketches are accurate enough to serve as blueprints that modern-day people could use to make models that work perfectly.

LEONARDO AND THE PLAGUE

During the summer of 1484, the bubonic plague arrived in Milan. This highly contagious disease often spread like wildfire in the cities it struck. People didn't know what caused the deadly disease, and there was no cure. Leonardo da Vinci didn't catch the plague, but he did use his scientific mind to think of possible solutions to the disease. He was convinced that pollution and waste in the city streets made the problem worse. After the plague killed off about one-third of Milan's population, Leonardo came up with a design for his ideal city. It would have wide streets to allow air to circulate freely. The city would also be cleaned frequently. Buildings would have fresh air vents. Would such a city have avoided the plague? We will never know since Leonardo's city was never built.

Leonardo tended to be a private person. He also kept much of his scientific thoughts to himself. And yet, he was tremendously prolific when it came to writing down his ideas, theories, and designs. Leonardo left thousands of pages of brilliant writings and drawings in his personal notebooks. Historians, scientists, and inventors have all benefitted from these notes.

Teacher and Father Figure

When Leonardo worked for the duke of Milan, he lived in his own space. A wing in a palace served as both his home and his workshop. Just as Verrocchio had acted as a mentor and teacher to the young Leonardo, so he provided the same guidance to his own students.

Apprentices, friends, and servants all buzzed about Leonardo's workshop. It was an exciting place full of new discoveries and artistic opportunities for the lucky students. Leonardo was known to be both brilliant and kind.

> **"Those who are obsessed with practice, but have no science, are like a pilot out with no tiller or compass . . . ."**
>
> **LEONARDO DA VINCI**

Among the friends Leonardo made in Milan was mathematician Luca Pacioli (1447–1517). The two met in 1496. Pacioli helped Leonardo expand his understanding of math. Pacioli was one of the very few people to whom Leonardo showed his notebooks.

BEATRIZ GALINDO

Beatriz Galindo was one of the most educated women of her time. Born around 1475 in Salamanca, Spain, she was a brilliant scholar of both Latin and the classics. Queen Isabella I hired Galindo to educate her and her children. Galindo was also made a personal advisor to the queen. In this male-dominated era, this was an incredible honor. Galindo also published works on poetry and classical authors.

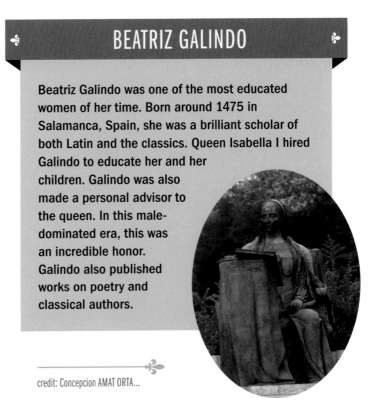

credit: Concepcion AMAT ORTA...

Pacioli and Leonardo spent lots of time discussing both math and art. Leonardo even helped illustrate Pacioli's book, titled *Divina Proportione*. Topics covered in this book include geometric studies of the polyhedron and capital letters.

Besides being a father figure to his students in Milan, Leonardo da Vinci adopted a 10-year-old boy named Giacomo (1480–1524). Giacomo was not a particularly well-behaved child. He stole, lied, and made lots of messes. According to Leonardo himself, the boy ate as much as two boys and caused as much trouble as four!

51

Leonardo nicknamed his son Salaì, which meant "demon." But no matter the mischief Salaì caused, Leonardo was quite fond of his son. He even taught Salaì to paint. The boy stayed with Leonardo for decades.

Moving Around

In 1499, the French invaded Milan. Leonardo's boss, the duke of Milan, was overthrown, so Leonardo had to pack up all his possessions and move. In December 1499, Leonardo left Milan with Salaì and Lucas Pacioli.

❧ INCAS: MASTERS OF FIBER INVENTION ❧

South America's Inca civilization was home to brilliant inventors, many of whom lived during the European Renaissance. These inventors created incredible innovations using handy materials. Some designed boats made from reeds that can still be found sailing on Lake Titicaca. Others created weapons from fibers. It might seem unlikely, but an Inca fiber sling was strong enough to split a sword made of steel! And centuries before there were any suspension bridges in Europe, the Incas had them. Yep, 500 years ago, the Incas could cross gorges or rivers on bridges made of—you guessed it—twisted mountain grass and other types of vegetation. There is still an Incan grass bridge left near the town of Huinchiri, Peru. Every year, this bridge gets rebuilt as part of an annual festival. People living in nearby villages help harvest the grasses and weave them into rope for the bridge construction. Amazing!

Leonardo traveled to different Italian cities after leaving Milan. He visited Mantua in February and Venice in March. While in Venice, Leonardo gave military advice to the city's governing council. Then, he returned to his family's native Florence.

> "It has long since come to my attention that people of accomplishment rarely sat back and let things happen to them. They went out and happened to things."
>
> **LEONARDO DA VINCI**

Leonardo spent the rest of his life moving from place to place. Where he lived depended on who his patron was or what project he was working on.

In the summer of 1502, Leonardo left Florence to work for Cesare Borgia (1475–1507), a notorious warlord who wanted to conquer city-states across Italy. It may seem odd that Leonardo decided to work for Borgia. After all, Leonardo was known for being a peace-loving kind of guy. Many sources say he was a vegetarian, known to buy birds at markets only to set them free. But everyone needs money!

Working for Cesare Borgia did have its perks. Leonardo's job as an engineer and military architect allowed him to meet scholars and visit libraries throughout Italy. Leonardo traveled for several months across Borgia's territories, surveying these lands and sketching topographical maps and city plans. Leonardo's maps were more accurate and detailed than maps created by other cartographers.

WONDER WHY?

Do you imagine that Leonardo's life would have been different if he had been independently wealthy and did not need the support of patrons? If yes, how so?

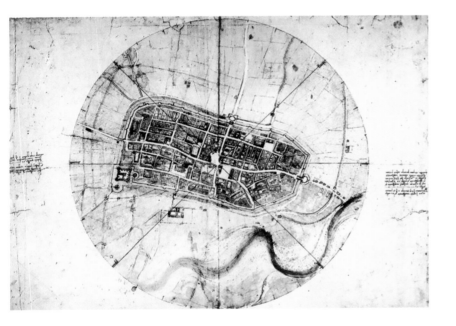

This great artist and scientist dissected human bodies to gain in-depth knowledge of the subject. He made many pen-and-ink drawings in his notebook of an old man who had died sometime during the winter of 1507–8. Leonardo dissected this man and carefully recorded his observations on paper.

A town plan of Imola by Leonardo, circa 1502

Leonardo returned to Florence in the spring of 1503. In addition to beginning his famous painting of the *Mona Lisa*, the ever-curious Renaissance man engaged in lots of scientific study during this period. He researched the physical properties of water. But perhaps Leonardo's best-known scientific pursuit of this period is his study of human anatomy.

CONNECT

Leonardo made intricate anatomical sketches. Take a look in this video!

🔍 Khan Leonardo anatomist

Leonardo's Final Years

From 1508 to 1513, Leonardo lived in Milan. He had very generous patrons there, including Charles d'Amboise (1473–1511) and King Louis XII (1462–1515). He made several anatomical discoveries. For example, he found out that the human heart has four chambers—up to that time, people believed it had only two. Leonardo's manuscripts from this period also feature botanical, geologic, mechanical, optical, and mathematical studies.

WONDER WHY?

If Leonardo were alive today, what twenty-first-century inventions do you think he would be most fascinated by? Why?

Political events in 1513 led to yet another move for Leonardo when the French were temporarily kicked out of Milan. Leonardo headed to Rome to work for a new patron, Giuliano de' Medici (1479–1516). This patron was the brother of Pope Leo X (1475–1521). Da Vinci was able to have his own suite of rooms in the Vatican and a good monthly stipend.

> **"Drawing seems to have been almost second nature to him."**
>
> SERGE BRAMLY (1949–), *LEONARDO: THE ARTIST AND THE MAN*

THE MEDICI FAMILY

During the Renaissance, many artists and architects earned their livelihoods from wealthy people known as patrons. A patron is someone who gives financial or other support to another person or cause. A patron might hire an architect to design a house or a painter to create a portrait of a family member. The Medici family was a very rich family in Italy during the Renaissance. They were merchants and bankers. They also held important government positions in Florence. The Medicis were most powerful during the 1400s and 1500s. They commissioned buildings, statues, paintings, and more. Members of the Medici family supported many famous artists, including Leonardo da Vinci.

During his days at the Vatican, Leonardo kept a low profile. He worked on mathematical studies and scientific experiments. He also continued his studies of plants. The Vatican's incredible gardens were a terrific resource for someone interested in botany.

Leonardo also drew up sketches for a huge residence for the Medici family in Florence. Like many of his other ideas, this one never came to fruition.

Perhaps Leonardo was frustrated that his architectural plans for the Medici home didn't pan out. Maybe he was upset he'd been banned from Santo Spirito Hospital, where he'd been doing human dissections. He was accused of practicing sorcery or magic by calling upon the spirits of the dead bodies he was working with.

Regardless of the reason, Leonardo left Italy for good by the close of 1516. He headed to France.

The young King Francis I (1494–1547) was his new patron. This king greatly respected Leonardo and treated him very well. Officially, Leonardo served as "first painter, architect, and engineer to the King."

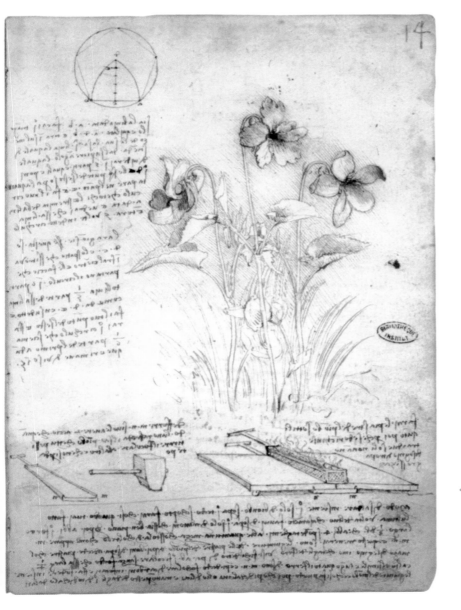

Botanical studies by Leonardo, circa 1490

Occasionally, the artist would create sketches for court festivals or even draw up architectural plans. But mostly, Leonardo continued his scientific studies.

In his final years, Leonardo suffered from some health problems, including arthritis and failing eyesight. In 1519, the great Leonardo da Vinci died at Cloux, a small residence near King Francis's summer palace at Amboise. He was 67 years old.

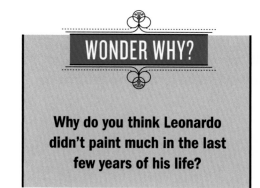

WONDER WHY?

Why do you think Leonardo didn't paint much in the last few years of his life?

Pages from one of Leonardo's notebooks

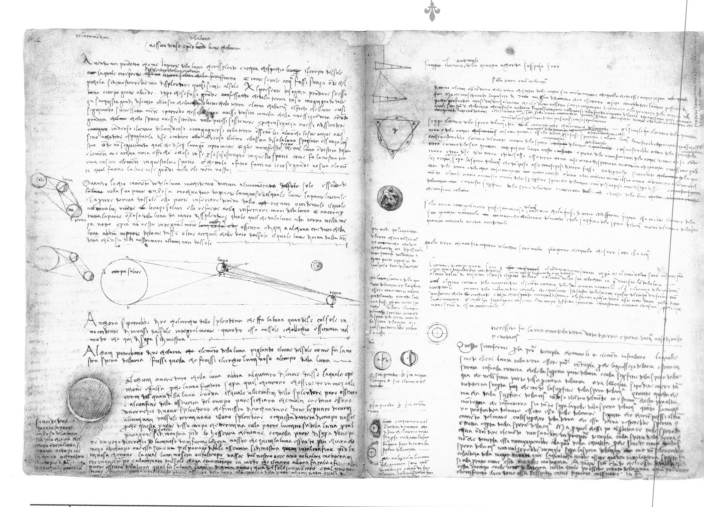

What Makes Him Different?

Leonardo da Vinci was unlike other Renaissance inventors. For one thing, many of his inventions were way ahead of their time, meaning that the technology to make them function properly was not available when he was alive. Examples include the helicopter, airplane, and a diving apparatus.

CONNECT

The British Library has an amazing website where people can view and even turn the pages of Leonardo's notebook. Do you keep a journal? How are journals helpful to scientists, engineers, and other thinkers?

🔍 British Library turning page

Another way that Leonardo was different from other inventors of the time was his education. While many other celebrated Renaissance inventors were provided with excellent academic opportunities, Leonardo was not. Much of his extensive knowledge of science came through self-study and constant hands-on experimentation and research.

> "I have offended God and mankind because my work did not reach the quality it should have."
>
> **LEONARDO DA VINCI**

Lasting Legacy

Leonardo da Vinci might be the best-known scientist-artist of the Renaissance. His paintings, such as the *Mona Lisa* and *The Last Supper*, continue to thrill art lovers. He is known for combining his skill as an engineer with his artistic talent. His notebooks offered ideas about many fields of study, from botany to architecture. Many of his inventions came to fruition centuries after Leonardo's death. And he provided incredible advances to our knowledge of human anatomy.

WORDS OF WONDER

What vocabulary words did you discover? Can you figure out the meanings of these words by using the context and roots? Look in the glossary for help!

anatomy · elite · ornithopter
pigments · polyhedron · topographical

Build a Parachute

Leonardo da Vinci invented a parachute made of linen cloth and wooden poles. In his notebook, the inventor states that a person who used this parachute could jump from any height without injury. You can see his sketch—along with other sketches—at this website. Try building a smaller version with the steps below!

 history stack da Vinci amazing drawings

> **Sketch your own design for a parachute, based on Leonardo's drawing.** Decide what materials might be best to use. Paper? Cloth? What about materials for the frame?

> **Gather materials and build a prototype.** See if you can create a parachute just like the one Leonardo drew. How would someone attach themselves to the parachute?

> **Test your prototype by attaching a figurine to the parachute with string.** Find a safe place to drop the parachute without hitting anyone.

> **Perform the drop!** What happens? Does the parachute work? What improvements can you make to the design? What happens as you add more weight?

CONNECT

In 2000, a man named Adrian Nicholas built and tested a parachute based on Leonardo's designs. You can watch him at this website.

Adrian Nicholas da Vinci parachute

Mirror Writing

Leonardo da Vinci often wrote backward in his notebooks, beginning at the right side of the page and moving toward the left. Why? Some think he did this to keep his hands clean—he was left-handed. Remember, ink in Leonardo's time was easily smudged. Try writing backward and then reading it in a mirror.

> ➤ **Begin by trying to write your signature backward.** It should be in cursive writing.

> ➤ **Having trouble making letters backward?** Here's an activity to try: Place a pencil in each hand. With the hand you usually write with, try writing the name of your town backward. At the same time, use the hand you normally don't write with and write the name of your town forward. This activity may help your brain coordinate the movements of your two hands.

> ➤ **Experiment with writing the alphabet backward.** Try writing the name of your favorite musician.

> ➤ **Try writing backward with markers or pens.** Are these tools any easier to work with?

> ➤ **Use a mirror to see if you can read the backward writing you created.** Did you reverse all the letters correctly?

> ➤ **You can try sending a secret message to a friend and letting your friend decode it using a mirror.** Have fun!

CONNECT

The Boston Museum of Science website lets you type a message that it turns into mirror writing.

🔍 **Museum of Science mirror writing**

A portrait of Mercator by Frans Hogenberg, from the *Atlas sive Cosmographicae Meditationes de Fabrica Mundi et Fabricati Figura*, 1574

CHAPTER 4

GERARDUS
Mercator

FAST FACTS

When you try to draw a spherical world on a flat map, you can never quite manage a completely accurate representation of the land. Gerardus Mercator came up with a solution that was so good, we still use it today!

BIRTH DATE:
MARCH 5, 1512

PLACE OF BIRTH:
RUPELMONDE IN FLANDERS, IN MODERN-DAY BELGIUM

AGE AT DEATH: 82 (DIED DECEMBER 2, 1594)

FAMOUS ACCOMPLISHMENT: HE CAME UP WITH A POPULAR MAP PROJECTION SHOWING THE SPHERICAL EARTH ON A FLAT SURFACE.

An image from Mercator's 1551 globe

Gerardus Mercator was a cartographer and geographer. His depiction of the globe became one of the most influential in history. Mercator's projection from 1569 was adopted as the standard used for nautical purposes.

Mercator's Childhood

On March 5, 1512, a baby was born who would change the way people looked at the world. This baby, named Gerard Kremer, is known to people today as Gerardus Mercator. He was born in a hospice in the city of Rupelmonde. A hospice was a place where travelers could find lodging and food.

Mercator's father, Hubert Kremer, was a cobbler who also worked as a farmer. Mercator's mother's name was Emerentia. Baby Mercator was the seventh and last child born to his parents.

A few weeks after his birth, the Kremer family went back to their hometown of Gangelt, in western Germany near the country's border with what is now the Netherlands.

When Mercator was a young boy, his family was poor. Just keeping food on the table was often a struggle. Mercator's diet was mostly made up of bread. In 1518, after a number of bad harvest seasons, Mercator's family left Gangelt and returned to Rupelmonde to seek new opportunities.

This move turned out to be a wise decision. Mercator's uncle Gisbert was well-connected and the family had more money. Mercator started school not long after arriving in Rupelmonde and studied arithmetic, Latin, and theology. It's said that by the time young Mercator was seven, he could both speak and read Latin fluently.

Portrait of mapmakers Gerard Mercator and Jodocus Hondius **by Colette Hondius Keere, 1613**

Gerardus Mercator
1512–1594

1512
Gerard Kremer, later Gerardus Mercator, is born in Rupelmonde, Flanders, on March 5, 1512.

1530–32
Mercator attends the University of Louvain.

1536
Mercator marries Barbara Schellekens.

1536
Gemma Frisius and Mercator create a printed terrestrial globe.

GERARDUS MERCATOR NATUS RUPELMUNDÆ III NON. MARTII ANNO CIƆIƆXII: VIXIT ANN. LXXXII. M. VIII. D. XXVI: DENATUS IV NON. DECEMBRIS ANNO CIƆIƆXCIV.

IUDOCUS HONDIUS NATUS IN PAGO FLANDRIÆ DICTO WACKENE XVI KALEND. NOVEMBRIS ANNO CIƆIƆLXIII: VIXIT ANN. XLVII. M. VII. D. XXIX: DENATUS XIV KAL. MARTII ANNO CIƆIƆCXII.

1538
Mercator produces a world map using a double cordiform projection.

1544
The Inquisition unjustly imprisons Mercator for seven months.

1564
Mercator creates a detailed and very accurate map of England, Scotland, and Ireland.

1569
Mercator develops a world map using his new projection.

1589
The first volume of Mercator's atlas is published.

1594
Mercator dies in Duisberg, in modern-day Germany.

Rupelmonde was an exciting city in the early 1500s. Barges brought goods such as wheat, firewood, even satin and silk to the wharves here. As people came in on the River Schelde, news from overseas also arrived, including stories of the travels of Amerigo Vespucci (1454–1512), Christopher Columbus (1436–1506), and Vasco da Gama (c. 1460–1524).

"Mercator knew Palestine better than any place outside the Low Countries. He had grown up with its miracles and revelations. He knew its history. Palestine had been the subject of the first map that most of his generation had ever seen."

CRANE 2003

Despite the adventures of Renaissance explorers, Mercator's experience of the world to that point was flat. After all, the area where he lived was not full of high peaks or dramatic landscapes that were unfolding to the explorers of the time. However, Mercator would learn much about the shape of the world in the decades to come.

Sad Times and New Opportunities

Dramatic events were taking place in Mercator's world. For one thing, many people were unhappy with the Catholic Church. Some questioned how it was being run. Others disagreed with the Church's teachings.

Martin Luther (1483–1546), a German priest, started to criticize the Catholic Church publicly. Luther's actions sparked a movement known as the Protestant Reformation. During this time, many Europeans left the Catholic Church and converted to Protestantism.

Young Mercator's life was full of drama, too. In 1526, his father died. And just a few years later, so did his mother. Luckily, his kind uncle Gisbert took responsibility for Mercator and made sure the clever teenage boy continued his education.

WONDER WHY?

Do you write in cursive? Was it difficult to learn? How is cursive useful?

A DAY IN THE LIFE

A group called the Brethren of the Common Life ran Mercator's school. The students divided their time between the school in the town center and the Brethren house where they lived. The students had to speak Latin all the time. Girls, alcohol, and even owning personal property were against the rules. The boys wore hooded gray outfits. On weekdays, lessons began at 6 a.m. and students attended two sessions of Mass during the day. It was a serious environment where one could get an excellent education. But it wasn't a place for fun!

When he was 15, Mercator went to school in a town called 's-Hertogenbosch, today located in the Netherlands. This religious school accepted boys who were bright but poor. The brothers who taught here were known for copying sacred texts.

In addition to studying Latin and Christian theology, Mercator learned elegant penmanship. His interest in beautiful writing lasted a lifetime.

St. John's cathedral, in the town where Mercator went to school as a teen

credit: Ingo Ronner (CC BY 2.0)

University Years

After more than three years as a student in 's-Hertogenbosch, Mercator had learned a lot. In 1530, because of his excellent effort, he got a scholarship to attend the University of Louvain in what's now Belgium. During this period, Gerard changed his name to Gerardus Mercator. It was common for students at the time to take on Latinized versions of their given names.

The University of Louvain was a terrific place to be a student. Founded in 1425, it was a well-established intellectual center by the time Mercator arrived. Students went there from all over Europe. Mercator lived in a dormitory and was enrolled in a two-year Faculty of Arts course, which took place in a teaching house known as the Castle.

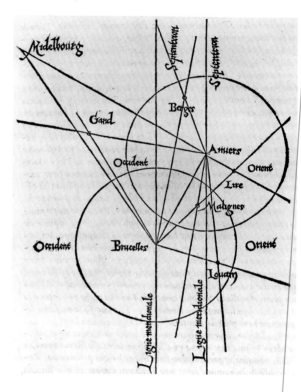

Triangulation by Gemma Frisius, 1553

TRIANGULATION

Dutch cartographer Gemma Frisius (1508–1555) developed a method of surveying known as triangulation, which is still used today. Triangulation is a way to determine the location of a place by forming triangles to it from other places with known locations. If geographers know the distance between two fixed points on the land, they can use math to help them find the location of another place—with an imaginary triangle that connects the three points.

During his time at Louvain, Mercator studied many different subjects. At first, he spent his time learning about logic. He also studied physics and philosophy. In 1532, Mercator graduated from the University of Louvain.

He continued to devote himself to learning after graduation. He studied theology, philosophy, and mathematics. He also worked to master a kind of writing script called italic. This script was clear and compressed. Mercator used italic script on maps he created later in life. Decades later, he even published a book on script.

A huge influence on Mercator was a brilliant scholar at Louvain named Gemma Frisius. Frisius was an expert in the areas of math, geography, and astronomy. He also made globes, maps, and other navigational equipment.

Mercator took a workshop with Frisius. He learned a great deal by working with the master, as well as with a local engraving expert named Gaspar Van der Heyden (1496–1549). Mercator learned how to print maps using engraved copperplates. These plates could make maps much more detailed than those in the past.

Mercator and Making Maps

Mercator worked with Frisius and Van der Heyden to make globes, maps, and other astronomical instruments for rich patrons. Mercator and Frisius collaborated to create a printed globe sometime around 1536. This was a terrestrial globe—the kind of globe you see in classrooms all over the world today.

How did people make globes back in Mercator's time? This 1536 globe had a spherical papier-mâché shell at its center. On top of the shell, Frisius's team pasted 12 separate printed gores, which were triangle-shaped, tapered pieces of cloth. Mercator engraved the italic lettering.

A view of the terrestrial globe of Gemma Frisius, Gerardus Mercator, and Gaspar Van der Heyden.

By the time he was 24, Mercator was already "a superb engraver, an outstanding calligrapher, and one of the leading scientific instrument makers of his time."

CONNECT

You can view Mercator's terrestrial globe at this website. Why might some of the land shapes be different from those on contemporary globes?

🔍 Harvard Mercator terrestrial globe

Gerardus Mercator experienced more than professional success. In August 1536, he married a woman named Barbara Schellekens. She delivered their first child, Arnold, in 1537. Eventually, the couple had three daughters and three sons.

The late 1530s and early 1540s were a productive time for Mercator. In 1537, he and his colleagues completed a celestial globe. Celestial globes show the locations of stars and constellations in the sky. Because Mercator was such a quick learner, he did more than just the engraving on the globe. In fact, he was considered a coauthor on this globe. Impressive!

Besides his work on globes, Mercator also published his own map of Palestine in 1537. He was fascinated by theology and the Bible, and Palestine was where things happened in the Bible. Mercator printed the map as six separate sheets, but when glued together, they made a wall-sized map. This map was commercially successful and stayed in print for more than four decades.

CONNECT

You can look at Mercator's celestial globe at this website. What do you notice about it?

🔍 Harvard Mercator celestial globe

Mercator had another big year in 1538. He published a world map on a unique projection called double cordiform. You might describe it as double heart-shaped. Mercator didn't invent this projection. A French mathematician named Oronce Finé (1494–1555) created it in 1531, but Mercator improved on it.

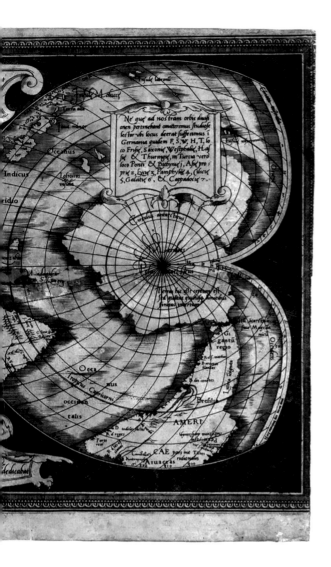

Mercator's 1538 world map. Do you see the double hearts?

However, no projection is perfect. It's very difficult to represent the spherical shape of Earth on a flat map. Mercator's 1538 double heart map was tough to read. One side of the heart-shaped projection showed the North Pole. The other showed the South Pole. People found it challenging to visualize the parts of the world in relation to one another. It was hard to see how Asia and North America were related to each other.

THE NORTHWEST PASSAGE

Imagine sailing in frigid waters through a series of channels with ice towering above you on both sides. This was the Northwest Passage. For centuries, beginning in the 1500s, explorers tried to find a route through the Arctic region that connected the North Atlantic and the Pacific Ocean to be used for faster trading. Why was it so difficult that it was 1906 before a ship was able to make the entire passage by sea? Icebergs that could rise hundreds of feet above the surface of the ocean and masses of ice that could trap ships for months at a time made this region nearly impossible to navigate. However, in 2017, the entire route stayed ice free thanks to climate change and warming temperatures.

Mercator's double heart map of 1538 was the first map that identified North America and South America as two separate continents. This map also suggested the possibility of a Northwest Passage. Mercator did his own research to make this map as accurate as he could, reflecting new discoveries of the time.

Going to Jail

Gerardus Mercator published a detailed map of Flanders in 1540. And the next year, he created the biggest printed globe that people had ever seen! Everything seemed to be going well for Mercator. But things were about to change.

During the sixteenth century, Flanders was often caught in conflict between Catholic traditionalists and Protestant reformers. Mercator's name was on a list of suspects wanted by agents of the Catholic Church known as inquisitors.

The Inquisition was first established to squash heretics. These were people who held beliefs that were in conflict with the teachings of the Roman Catholic Church. But in 1542, the Inquisition was working to crack down on Protestants.

Scholars debate why Mercator was the target of the inquisitors. Many don't even agree whether he was Catholic or Protestant. Some say he was targeted because of letters he wrote to Franciscan friars in Mechelen, Flanders. Others mention that Mercator did not accept the biblical version of how the universe was created.

Regardless of the reason, Gerardus Mercator was arrested in Rupelmonde. In 1544, Mercator was put in prison. After several months, he was finally released. It seemed that the inquisitors could not find evidence against Mercator. Many of his fellow prisoners did not fare so well. Some were burned at the stake, buried alive, beheaded, or banished.

Gerardus Mercator was imprisoned in Rupelmonde Castle. Visitors today can climb the tower here.

After what Mercator called his "most unjust persecution," he created a spectacular celestial globe in 1551. The next year, he left Louvain for what he hoped would be a more harmonious place to live and work.

Mercator's 1551 celestial globe

credit: Ulrichulrich

Mercator Moves to Germany

In 1552, Mercator moved to a place named Duisburg. Today, this city is part of Germany, but in Mercator's day it was located in the Duchy of Cleves. The duke of Cleve, William, had planned to start a university in Duisberg and offered Mercator a job. While this plan didn't work out, Mercator still had plenty of work making maps, globes, and various scientific instruments.

WONDER WHY?

Many mapmakers, including Mercator, employed women as colorists to enhance the appearance of their engravings. Why do you think the women didn't design the maps? Can you find out more about female cartographers today?

While in Duisberg, Mercator established a cartographic workshop. He had a staff of engravers to help with his various projects. One of the great works of this period was a 1564 map of England, Scotland, and Ireland. It's still celebrated for its accuracy.

Mercator's Revolutionary Projection

During the 1560s, Mercator continued to make globes and maps. But he wasn't satisfied with how vast distances were represented on large maps. The methods of projection used at the time resulted in maps that were distorted.

THE INQUISITION

During the thirteenth century, the Roman Catholic Church established a court known as the Inquisition. This court examined people who'd been accused of heresy, or gone against the teachings of the church. Inquisitors were officials in charge of questioning people. While inquisitors did offer accused people a chance to confess, they also were known to torture people to score such confessions. At times, innocent folks confessed because of the torture. What happened to those who did not confess? They were put on trial. If deemed guilty, the punishment could be fines, jail, or even death. Among the famous victims of the Inquisition are Joan of Arc (1412–1431), a French heroine, and Italian scientist Galileo Galilei, about whom you will learn in the next chapter. The Inquisition lasted into the nineteenth century.

It was nearly impossible for a navigator to plot his ship's course simply by using such a map. As a result, ships often got lost. Mapmakers also had a tough time accurately showing newly discovered lands on their maps.

So, what did Gerardus Mercator do? What any great inventor does—he got creative and found a solution to the problem. Mercator developed a new type of projection for his now-famous world map from 1569.

> "When I saw that Moses' version of the Genesis of the world did not fit sufficiently in many ways with Aristotle and the rest of the philosophers, I began to have doubts about the truth of all philosophers and started to investigate the secrets of nature."
>
> **GERARDUS MERCATOR**

CONNECT

In March 2015, Google in Belgium honored Mercator with a Google Doodle! Check it out!

 Mercator Google Doodle

MERCATOR THE MATH TEACHER

Today, when people think of Gerardus Mercator, they imagine his famous maps and globes. But did you know that he also worked as a math teacher? A new school had been founded in Duisberg, with classes beginning in October 1559. Mercator volunteered his services as a math teacher, but he made his curriculum more diverse than just math problems. He also taught his pupils about geography and cosmography. He used Gemma Frisius's texts to teach arithmetic and geometry. Mercator also brought his students outdoors to practice surveying and astronomy. Was his class a success? Yes. And the city council is even said to have given the great Mercator three fattened pigs instead of money as payment.

Of all the works created in his Duisberg workshop, this projection is probably the most celebrated. What was so special about Mercator's projection?

Straight lines on the map represented lines of constant direction on Earth's actual surface. The idea was that it would allow seamen to accurately plot a course of travel from one location to another. Of course, it needed to be used with other navigational tools that would take two centuries to invent, so his map wasn't immediately useful. Eventually, though, with the aid of these tools, a navigator could follow a course they'd charted on Mercator's map.

WONDER WHY?

Mercator did not spend any time at sea, yet he was committed to figuring out a way to help sailors navigate the ocean. Why? Where might passion like that come from if not personal interest?

Mercator's 1569 world map accurately depicted both the directions and shapes of landmasses. This map also let sailors see where the coastlines wound in and out. This was a real boon to Renaissance sailors, who didn't have the luxury of GPS or Google Earth! Mercator perfected what is now known as the Mercator projection. It was revolutionary, and became the standard projection used for nautical journeys.

Funnily enough, Gerardus Mercator himself never spent any time at sea!

Mercator's 1569 world map composite of all 18 sheets. Can you spot familiar land masses?

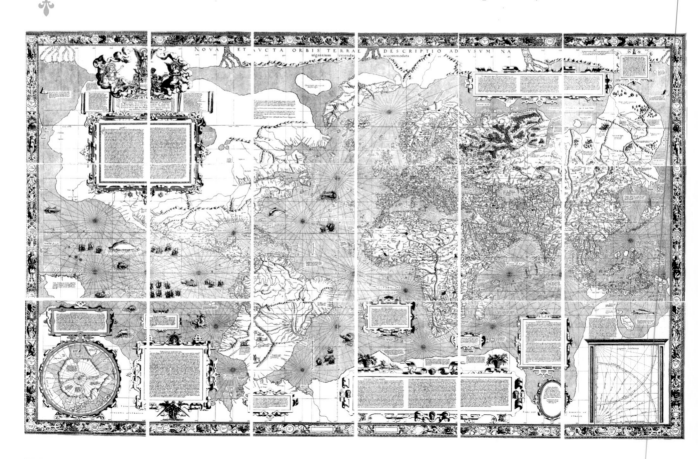

Mercator's 1595 map of the Arctic

Later Years

Gerardus Mercator worked on cartographic projects for the rest of his life. Even though he didn't do on-the-ground mapping, he sought out the most up-to-date geographical information by asking many correspondents to help him out. He used his skills as both a calligrapher and a mathematician to present all information both attractively and graphically on his maps.

CRITICISMS OF MERCATOR PROJECTION

By most accounts, Mercator's 1569 world map was his best-known work. Was it a perfect projection? Absolutely not! Since Mercator published this map, there have been a number of criticisms of it. The Mercator projection distorts both the size of nations and continents. This distortion increases as one moves farther from the equator on the map. For example, on Mercator's map, Greenland looks to be about the same size as the continent of Africa. But in reality, about 14 Greenlands could fit in Africa. Plus, the Mercator projection seems to support a particular worldview. North America and Europe appear much larger than they really are, which has led some critics to suggest it reinforces the view that those continents are superior to others.

"Since my youth, geography has been for me the primary object of study. While I was engaged in it, having applied the considerations of the natural and geometric sciences, I liked, little by little, not only the description of the earth, but also the structure of the whole machinery of the world, whose numerous elements are not known by anyone to date."

GERARDUS MERCATOR

Around 1571, the man who served as tutor to the heir to the Duchy of Cleves asked Mercator for good maps of Europe because he was getting ready for a tour of the continent.

Mercator worked hard to produce these maps. He went so far as to cut up maps he'd already created and make them suitable for a book format. He drew scale bars by hand and added titles.

Eventually, Mercator's atlas was published in two volumes. The British Library says these were published in 1589 and 1596. His son Rumold and three grandsons completed the project after his death.

CONNECT

You can examine Mercator's atlas of Europe, held at the British Library, at this website. How is it different from today's published atlases? How is it similar?

🔍 BL Mercator atlas Europe

In 1590 and 1593, Mercator had strokes, which paralyzed him and left him nearly blind. In 1594, another stroke took Mercator's life. He was 82 years old.

Lasting Legacy

Gerardus Mercator was one of the Renaissance's best-known geographers and mapmakers. The new projection he used in his 1569 world map was a huge advance for navigators. Using this map, they could chart a ship's course much more accurately than previous projections had allowed.

Mercator's many maps improved the geographical knowledge of many Renaissance people, from scholars to travelers. His atlas continues to thrill map-lovers around the world.

A MATTER OF PERSPECTIVE

When people think of famous maps from the Renaissance, many think of Mercator's famous projection. But Europeans weren't the only cartographers at this time. Korean astronomer Kwon Kun led a team to create a striking map from 1402. This map shows Europe as a tiny piece of land. India is also hardly visible. But China is shown as an enormous landmass in the center of the map. Korea is disproportionately large. Scholars today believe that perhaps the size of the various landmasses vary depending on how the areas were perceived politically by the Koreans. Do you think this is an issue with today's maps?

A front page in Mercator's 1595 atlas

ATLAS
SIVE
COSMOGRAPHICÆ
MEDITATIONES
DE
FABRICA MVNDI ET
FABRICATI FIGVRA.

Gerardo Mercatore Rupelmundano,
Illustrissimi Ducis Iulie Clivie & Mo̅
tis &c̅. Cosmographo Autore
Cum Privilegio

WORDS OF WONDER

What vocabulary words did you discover? Can you figure out the meanings of these words by using the context and roots? Look in the glossary for help!

hospice
Inquisition
italic
reformers
projection

WONDER WHY?

What are some of the different map projections used today? What are the advantages and disadvantages of each one?

Citrus Fruit Projections

Making a map of the spherical Earth on a flat surface can be tricky. Try it yourself and see how it turns out. This activity shows the difficulty Mercator faced in creating an accurate map projection.

> ➤ **Using a globe for reference, use a permanent marker to draw the seven continents on the surface of a grapefruit.** Don't stress if it's not perfect.

> ➤ **Let the ink dry thoroughly.**

> ➤ **Carefully peel your grapefruit.** Try to have as few pieces of peel as you can. Place the peeled grapefruit on a paper towel to eat later.

> ➤ **Try to lay the peel flat on another paper towel.** With your pencil, try to draw a map based on what your flattened peel looks like. Fill in any blank spaces where the peel is not covering the paper towel using your colored pen or marker.

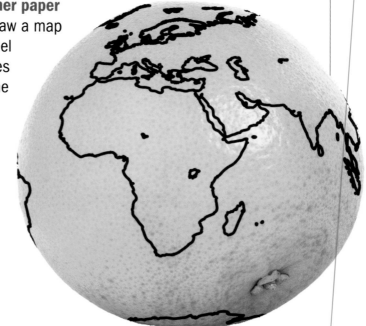

> ➤ **How is the map you drew on the grapefruit different from what came out on the paper?** Are some parts of your map more distorted than others?

Making a Map

In this activity, you'll use a Mercator projection to create a map of items in your house. You might be surprised at how far afield your belongings come from! For this activity, you can use a globe or print out a blank Mercator projection world map that you can find online.

➤ **Set a timer for 30 minutes.** Go from room to room in your house looking for items that come from different countries. Try to find items from the following categories: toys, foods, clothes, household items, and school supplies. Do you have any T-shirts from China? Any spices from Mexico? Olive oil from Italy?

➤ **Each time you find an item that is not from the country where you live, write down what the item is and where it's from.**

➤ **When the timer goes off, label all the countries where you found things from on a map.** Use the globe or world map to help you find the locations of countries you might not know.

➤ **Use red to shade in the countries where you found toys.** Use blue for foods. Use yellow for clothes. Use green for household items or school supplies.

➤ **Which items came from farthest away?** Do you see any pattern to where certain categories of items, such as clothes, came from?

CONNECT

Why are there so many products made in other countries in your house? Watch this Crash Course video to learn more about global trade.

🔍 **Crash Course history trade**

CHAPTER 5

GALILEO
Galilei

Galileo's first telescopic drawings of the moon to be published

Galileo Galilei was one of the greatest astronomers in history. He was also a renowned philosopher and physicist during the sixteenth and seventeenth centuries. A prolific inventor, Galileo created many devices, including an early kind of thermometer, the sector, and the hydrostatic balance.

FAST FACTS

BIRTH DATE:
FEBRUARY 15, 1564

PLACE OF BIRTH:
PISA, ITALY

AGE AT DEATH: 77 (DIED JANUARY 8, 1642)

FAMOUS ACCOMPLISHMENT:
MANY, INCLUDING HIS DISCOVERY OF THE MOONS OF JUPITER

Galileo found connections and saw patterns in many different subjects. This expansive way of thinking helped him build his knowledge and make discoveries in whatever field his curiosity drew him.

Galileo's Childhood

Galileo Galilei was born in Pisa, Italy, on February 15, 1564. He was the oldest of six children. His father, Vincenzo Galilei, was a musician from Florence. His mother's name was Giulia Ammannati.

When Galileo was still a child, his father moved to Florence, probably to take part in something related to his work as a musician.

> "You cannot teach a man anything, you can only help him find it within himself."
>
> **GALILEO GALILEI**

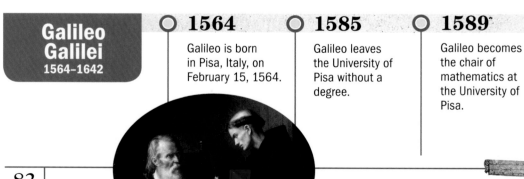

Galileo Galilei
1564–1642

1564
Galileo is born in Pisa, Italy, on February 15, 1564.

1585
Galileo leaves the University of Pisa without a degree.

1589
Galileo becomes the chair of mathematics at the University of Pisa.

1595–98
Galileo invents the sector.

Galileo started his education at a public school in Pisa, sometime between 1569 and 1574.

Near the end of 1574, Galileo moved to Florence, where he met up with his father. During this time, he studied Greek and the humanities. He also learned about drawing, music, and dialectics. It's said he was a talented lute player.

During the next chapter of his education, Galileo studied with the Vallombrosan monks. These monks were affiliated with the Roman Catholic Church. Notes from Galileo himself indicate that he studied logic.

In 1578, Galileo developed an eye infection. Some historians say it was a severe infection, while others claim it simply wasn't tended to properly. Either way, Galileo's father used the infection as an excuse to bring Galileo back to Florence— permanently.

RENAISSANCE WOMEN

Sophia Brahe was born in Knudstrup, Denmark, in 1556. Her older brother Tycho was a well-known astronomer. Even though it was not common for girls of the time, Brahe studied chemistry and horticulture. But Tycho told his young sister not to study astronomy. Did Brahe listen? Absolutely not! Instead, she used her own money to have astronomy books translated from Latin so she could read them. Brahe's brother was proud that she'd learned astronomy through her own efforts. When Brahe was just a teen, she started assisting Tycho with his work. In November 1572, she helped with astronomical observations that led to the discovery of a new star in the constellation Cassiopeia—that we now know was a supernova, or the massive explosion of a star. As she got older, Brahe continued her scientific studies and also wrote an important historical work on the Danish nobility. She was a true Renaissance woman!

Apparently, Vincenzo didn't like the influence the monks had over Galileo. The 15-year-old had announced that he planned to become a monk, but his father believed he should become a doctor instead.

1600	**1609**	**1610**	**1632**	**1633**	**1642**
Galileo has the first of three children with Marina Gamba.	Galileo builds several telescopes of improving quality.	Galileo publishes a book about astronomy titled *Starry Messenger*.	Galileo publishes *Dialogue Concerning the Two Chief World Systems: Ptolemaic and Copernican*.	Galileo is found guilty of heresy by the Inquisition. He remains under house arrest for the rest of his life.	Galileo dies in Arcetri, Italy, on January 8, 1642.

From Student to Author-Inventor

In 1580 or 1581, the teenage Galileo left Florence to study at the University of Pisa. At first, he took his father's advice and enrolled as a student of medicine. But medicine wasn't really his passion. Plus, his professors did not satisfy Galileo's curiosity. He preferred to conduct experiments and figure things out on his own, rather than just accept the teachings of his professors or ideas from the ancient Greek philosophers Aristotle and Plato.

After convincing his father that he wasn't interested in being a doctor, he changed his focus to study mathematics and philosophy.

In 1585, Galileo left Pisa and the university—without a degree. Some sources say he left because of financial problems. Despite leaving the university, Galileo continued his mathematical studies and made a living by teaching math in Florence and Siena. Even without a degree!

When he was just 22 years old, Galileo wrote his first scientific book. It was titled *The Little Balance*. At this time in Europe, jewelers commonly weighed precious metals such as gold or silver first in air and then in water to find their specific gravity.

Title page of Galileo Galilei's *Dialogue Concerning the Two Chief World Systems*

Published by Giovanni Battista Landini in 1632 in Florence. This book proved to be Galileo's downfall.

Why would they do this? Specific gravity is a measurement that was used to determine whether these metals were real or not. Galileo had some of his own ideas about how to improve or refine this practice. He shared these ideas in his book. Galileo carefully described a balance that could accurately weigh objects both in air and water. Today, this is known as a hydrostatic balance.

Galileo the Professor— and the Papa

In 1589, Galileo Galilei headed back to the University of Pisa. This time he wasn't a student—he was the chair of mathematics. What a change!

Galileo's father passed away in 1591. As the oldest son, it was now Galileo's job to financially support the other members of his family. Since his job at Pisa wasn't very well paid, he looked around for a higher-paying post. Luckily, he found one in Padua, Italy.

PIG NECK TOOTHBRUSH

Like brushing your teeth? Thank a Renaissance inventor from China! Around the globe, people brush their teeth every day. Ancient peoples often used a "chew stick," which was basically a skinny twig that had a frayed end. But during the Renaissance, the bristle toothbrush was invented in China. The year was 1498, but the clever Chinese inventor's name remains a mystery. This toothbrush's bristles were made of coarse, stiff hairs removed from the back of a pig's neck. The bristles were attached to a handle made of bamboo or bone. These boar or pig bristles remained the norm for toothbrushes until 1938, when nylon bristles came to be. Brushing your teeth might be a chore, but it could be worse!

Galileo gave his first lecture at the University of Padua in December 1592 and stayed for 18 years. Later, he would describe these years as the happiest ones of his life. He taught geometry to students. He also taught astronomy— the geocentric variety, where the earth is seen as the center of the universe.

"To understand the Universe, you must understand the language in which it's written, the language of Mathematics."

GALILEO GALILEI

Galileo Demonstrating the New Astronomical Theories at the University of Padua, 1873

By Felix Parra (1845–1919)

During his time in Padua, Galileo began a long-term relationship with a woman named Marina Gamba. Born in about 1570, she might have met the brilliant scientist during one of his frequent trips to Venice.

Galileo and Marina never married, perhaps because, like many ordinary people of the time, they could not afford to marry. They did have three children together, Virginia, born in 1600, Livia, the following year, and, in 1606, a son named Vincenzo.

WONDER WHY?

Do you or people you know have parents who aren't married? How are families viewed differently today than they were during the Renaissance?

Galileo did not officially acknowledge that he was the father of his children with Marina. Why? It was considered to be unwise for a few reasons.

+ He had friendships with some elite people, such as the Venetian nobility.

+ He had a prestigious job as a university professor.

+ He hadn't married Marina before they had kids together.

Galileo Galilei was a very productive scholar while at Padua. He worked on a number of different experiments. One of the best-known focused on falling objects.

Before Galileo came along, people believed that heavier objects fell more quickly than lighter ones. Have you seen this in action? What happens when you drop a tennis ball and a bowling ball from the same height? Which reaches the ground first?

Galileo studied how falling objects moved. He used ramps that would slow objects as they were falling. That allowed him to more carefully observe the objects in motion and collect data.

Galileo thought a ball that rolled down an incline would accelerate just like a free-falling object, except more slowly. Galileo used a device called an inclined plane. This was a straight piece of wood that had a gentle slope to it. It also had a groove running down its center.

By rolling a ball down this inclined plane, Galileo could slow the effect of gravity on the ball. This inclined plane made it possible for Galileo to measure acceleration accurately with simple instruments.

CONNECT

Want to learn more about inclined planes? Check out this video! You might think inclined planes are very simple, but there's a lot at work when a ball is rolling down an inclined plane!

🔍 **Udacity inclined planes**

Galileo also studied falling objects by conducting a famous experiment at the Leaning Tower of Pisa. Historians today debate whether this actually occurred. Back in Galileo's time, scientists did not write detailed reports to describe their experimental research.

"It is a beautiful and delightful sight to behold the body of the Moon."

GALILEO GALILEI

According to many sources, in the early 1590s, Galileo dropped balls of different weights from this tower. Why? To see whether a heavier ball would fall faster than a lighter one. While we don't know exactly how heavy the balls were or whether he definitely dropped them from this tower, we do know he conducted experiments to test the effects of gravity.

The inclined plane and Leaning Tower experiments both led to clear results. Galileo determined that without air resistance, gravity makes all objects fall at the same rate of speed. Today, this is known as the equivalence principle.

More Ideas and Inventions

Teacher. Researcher. Inventor. It seemed that Galileo Galilei never ran out of questions to ask or ideas to pursue. For example, during Galileo's life, cannons were regularly used in times of war. Since their introduction to Europe in 1325, these cannons had also become more mobile and sophisticated.

CONNECT

In 1971, astronaut David Scott (1932–) tested out Galileo's findings on the moon. He dropped a feather from one hand and a hammer from the other. The two objects hit the moon's surface at exactly the same time. Scott exclaimed, "What do you know! Mr. Galileo was right."

🔍 **Apollo 15 hammer feather**

But gunners—the people who fired the cannons—needed better instruments so they could coordinate and calculate the cannon firing. Here's where Galileo enters the scene.

Sometime between 1595 and 1598, Galileo designed what's known as a sector. This tool had two legs with useful scales engraved on them to help gunners make quick calculations as needed. It also had a plumb line to determine elevation.

The sector helped gunners figure out how much to elevate their cannons in battle to shoot more effectively. It also gave them a faster way to compute how much gunpowder they needed, depending on how big the cannonball was and what material it was made of.

Have you ever looked at a thermometer to see what the temperature outside was? Well, back in Galileo's time such a tool did not exist—at least, not as we know it today. So, he created his own version of a thermometer-like device called a thermoscope.

The basic idea behind the thermoscope was that air expanded when heat was present. Galileo's thermoscope was made of an egg-sized glass that had a long neck. Galileo would heat the jar using his hands. Then he would partially immerse the jar (upside down) in a container that was filled with water.

When Galileo removed his hands, the water would rise in the neck of the glass. This showed how temperature variations caused changes in air density.

In the following years, Galileo and some friends further refined the thermoscope into a true air thermometer with a numerical scale. However, it would be decades before there was a universal standard for measuring temperature!

GALILEO'S CHILDREN

Historians know that Galileo had three children with Marina Gamba. Galileo's two daughters, Virginia and Livia, never married. Some sources say Galileo believed they shouldn't marry since they'd been born to unmarried parents. Other sources say Galileo could not provide an acceptable dowry for his daughters. Without a dowry of property or money brought by a bride to her husband, many young women were unable to marry. Regardless of the reason, both of Galileo's daughters were sent to convents and became nuns. Virginia—considered to be Galileo's most gifted child—was just 13 when she entered the Convent of San Matteo in Arcetri, Florence. While in the convent, she became known as Maria Celeste. She corresponded with her father for many years. In their letters, Maria Celeste and her dad discussed topics from health to science to religion. Amazingly, 124 of these letters still survive. Livia, who took the name Arcangela at the convent, was described as silent and strange. Galileo's son, Vincenzio, moved to Florence with his dad when his mother Marina married another man. He ended up studying law at the University of Pisa. If Galileo had married Marina Gamba, do you think his children's lives would have been different?

A sector, invented by Galileo

He went on to compare two pendulums that were similar in length. He was able to demonstrate that they'd swing at the same speed, even if they were pulled at different lengths.

WONDER WHY?

Galileo was curious about lots of different things! What did this mean for his professional life? Are you naturally curious?

Telescopes and Travel

Galileo's recreated thermometer

credit: fenners

In Padua, Galileo also started researching pendulums. In 1602, he wrote a letter to a friend and explained some of his ideas about pendulums. He said that the amount of time it takes a pendulum to swing is not linked to its arc but rather to the length of the pendulum.

In 1609, Galileo got word about an invention that would change his life. It was the telescope, sometimes called a spyglass. Though Galileo is often credited with inventing the telescope, that isn't true. The first telescope was invented in Holland by a man named Hans Lippershey (1570–1619). When this device was invented, it was designed to "see faraway things as if nearby."

News of the spyglass spread quickly across Europe. Before Galileo ever saw one in person, he built his own, around June or July 1609. This was a three-powered one, meaning it could magnify things to three times their actual size. An eight-powered telescope soon followed. By October or November, he'd built a 20-powered telescope.

Galileo turned his new device to the heavens. He made many amazing astronomical discoveries. He observed the moon, including its valleys and mountains. He also discovered four moons of the planet Jupiter that were later named Io, Callisto, Europa, and Ganymede.

While today these are known as the Galilean satellites, Galileo referred to them as the "Medicean stars," in honor of Cosimo II de' Medici (1590–1621) and his three brothers. He also sent Cosimo an excellent quality telescope. Two smart political moves.

The moons of Jupiter, photographed by *Voyager 1*, 1998

credit: NASA/JPL

CONNECT

You can read a description of Galileo's discovery of the moons of Jupiter here. What might it have felt like to look at something no human eyes had ever seen before?

🔍 **Cengage Galileo Jupiter**

Galileo used his telescope to identify the various phases of Venus and to see sunspots. In May 1610, he published a short book about his astronomical discoveries titled the *Starry Messenger.*

Just a month later, Galileo Galilei gave up his post at Padua to work for Cosimo II de' Medici, the grand duke of Tuscany.

Galileo offering his telescope to three women, 1655

Artist unknown

credit: Retrieved from the Library of Congress

Troubled Times Ahead

Galileo was a scientific rock star. People treated him as a celebrity.

One might imagine that Galileo's life would have been smooth sailing as he continued to make incredible astronomical discoveries. But that wasn't the case. The more Galileo observed of space, the more he supported a view of the universe known as Copernicanism.

The Copernican model of the universe conflicted with the view held by the Catholic Church. The Church saw the earth, not the sun, as the center of the universe. Having witnessed Jupiter with its moons orbiting around it, perhaps the earth also moved, with its moon moving around it.

Disagreeing with the Church's beliefs was a bad idea though, and Galileo knew it.

NICOLAUS COPERNICUS

Nicolaus Copernicus (1473–1543) was a Polish astronomer, scientist, and mathematician. When he was 18 years old, he went to Italy to attend college. Part of his educational training included the study of astrology—reading the stars to learn about events of the future. Astronomy was also an essential part of such training. During Copernicus's life, most people believed that Earth was the center of the universe. They believed that the stars, the sun, and all the planets revolved around the earth. Copernicus had a different idea—that the sun was the center of the universe. He said that the planets orbited the sun, not the earth. When he was 70 years old, Copernicus published a book of his findings titled *On the Revolutions of the Heavenly Spheres*.

Nicolaus Copernicus, artist unknown (top)

Copernicus's diagram of a heliocentric cosmos (bottom)

So even though he privately supported Copernicus's model of the universe, Galileo tried to keep quiet. He chose not to make any public statements on this issue.

However, in 1616, Galileo wrote a letter to Christina, the grand duchess of Lorraine (1565–1637), that had serious consequences. In the letter, he clearly stated that the Copernican view of the universe was a physical reality. He argued that the Holy Scripture should not be interpreted literally when that interpretation contradicted facts proven by mathematical science.

> **"All truths are easy to understand once they are discovered; the point is to discover them."**
>
> **GALILEO GALILEI**

In 1616, the Catholic Church officially condemned Copernicus's teachings. The Church forbade Galileo from holding Copernican views on the universe.

Did Galileo actually change his views? No. When a new pope, who was a fan of Galileo's work, came into office, the scientist thought he was in the clear. His health wasn't good at this stage of his life. In February of 1632, Galileo published a work called *Dialogue Concerning the Two Chief World Systems: Ptolemaic and Copernican.*

WONDER WHY?

Why do you think Galileo continued to write and publish scientific works that he knew might lead to problems for himself? What does this say about his character?

The Inquisition banned the sale of this book not long after it was published. Galileo was ordered to Rome to appear before the Inquisition. At the end of his trial, Galileo was found guilty of heresy and sentenced to lifelong house arrest. As part of his punishment, Galileo also had to publicly withdraw his support of the Copernican theory.

Galileo worked for most of the time at his villa south of Florence in Arcetri. During his last years, he wrote up some of his mathematical works, including his ideas on the principles of mechanics and the laws of motion. These texts were smuggled out of Italy and published in Holland in 1638 as *Discourses Concerning Two New Sciences.*

Galileo also continued his studies of the pendulum. In 1641, he came up with a design for a pendulum clock.

Galileo with his telescope in the Piazza San Marco, Venice. Wood engraving.

Artist unknown

credit: Wellcome Collection

Lasting Legacy

Galileo Galilei, one of the most brilliant astronomers and scientists of the Renaissance, died on January 8, 1642, in Arcetri. His improvements to the telescope allowed him to make incredible new discoveries about the heavens, including finding the four moons of Jupiter.

Despite the problems it caused for him personally, Galileo's observations helped to convince people that the Copernican view of the solar system was correct.

In addition to his astronomical work, Galileo furthered peoples' knowledge of the motion of falling objects. He was also a creative inventor, coming up with new devices such as the sector and the hydrostatic balance.

WORDS OF WONDER

What vocabulary words did you discover? Can you figure out the meanings of these words by using the context and roots? Look in the glossary for help!

geocentric · hydrostatic · balance incline · sector · gravity

Falling Objects

In this activity, you will recreate Galileo's famous experiment at the Leaning Tower of Pisa. Will your findings match Galileo's?

> **Climb onto a step stool or a chair with two balls that are different weights.** It's a good idea to have someone hold onto the stool or chair to be sure it doesn't tip.

> **Have a partner get a timer ready.** Your partner should start the timer as soon as you drop the balls.

> **Drop the two balls at the same time from the same height.** Did they hit the ground at the same time? Or did one hit the ground before the other?

> **Record on a piece of paper the following information: Trial Number, Light Ball, Heavy Ball, Same Time.**

> **Repeat this experiment 8 to 10 times to be sure your findings are consistent.**

> **Try recording your experiment on a phone or video camera to see whether your balls hit the ground at the same time and how long they take to travel from your hands to the ground.** What information can you get from a slowed recording that you can't see with your own eyes?

CONNECT

What about a feather and a bowling ball? Will these two very distinct objects travel at the same rate? Check out this video that shows what happens when you drop a bowling ball and a feather in an airless room.

🔎 **feather bowling ball**

Make a Pendulum

Galileo experimented quite a bit with pendulums. For example, he observed the connection between the length of the pendulum's rope and the time it took to go back and forth. Make your own pendulum and record your observations!

> ➤ **Place a ruler at the end of a flat surface, such as a desk or table.** About 4 inches of the ruler should stick out over the end of this surface. Make sure that there is an open area under the ruler so the pendulum can swing freely.

> ➤ **Put a heavy book or bag of flour on top of the ruler so it stays in place.**

> ➤ **With a marker, make lines on a piece of string marking off 29.5 inches, 21 inches, and 13.5 inches.**

> ➤ **If your ruler has a hole in the end, tie one end of the string through it.** If not, just tie the string around the end of the ruler. Tie the loose end of the string around your weight.

> ➤ **Record the length of the string from the knot at the top of the ruler to the weight.** Have a timer ready.

> ➤ **Pull the weight to one side and let go.** Let your pendulum make 10 complete swings back and forth. Record the speed of the swings. How can you measure the length of the swings?

> ➤ **Now, cut the string to the 21-inch mark.** Reattach the weight. Repeat the directions for step 6 and record your findings. Try again after cutting the string to 13.5 inches.

> ➤ **How did your results vary depending on the length of the string?**

GLOSSARY

acceleration: moving faster, increasing in speed.

adapt: to make a change in response to new or different conditions.

air resistance: the force of air pushing against an object.

alloy: a substance made of two or more metals or of a metal and a nonmetal, usually melted together.

anatomy: the branch of science focused on the bodily structure of humans, animals, and other organisms.

anemometer: an instrument used to measure wind speed.

antimony: a metallic silvery element often used in alloys and medicine.

apprentice: a person who learns a job or skill by working for someone who is good at it.

arc: a curved path.

architecture: the style or look of a building.

artifact: an object made by a human being.

artisan: someone who is skilled at a craft.

astronomy: the study of the sun, moon, stars, planets, and space.

atlas: a book of maps or charts.

banish: to send someone away from a country or place as an official punishment.

BCE: put after a date, BCE stands for Before Common Era and counts down to zero. CE stands for Common Era and counts up from zero. These non-religious terms correspond to BC and AD. This book was printed in 2018 CE.

blacksmithing: the job of a blacksmith, which is working to shape metal into useful tools.

block printing: a printing process where images are carved in reverse into a large piece of wood, then inked and pressed onto paper.

boarding school: a school where students live during the school term.

botanical: related to the study of plants.

bronze: a hard metal created by combining copper and tin.

brothers: male members of a religious order.

bubonic plague: a deadly infectious disease carried by rats and mice that can spread to humans. Also called Black Death.

calligraphy: beautiful writing or fancy lettering.

canon law: the branch of law dealing with the church, especially the laws made by the pope.

cartographer: a person who makes maps.

cast: a model of a shape, such as a letter or footprint, made by pouring liquid into a mold and letting it harden.

celestial: positioned in or relating to the sky.

cipher wheel: a wheel-shaped tool used for creating messages in a secret way.

circumnavigation: sailing or otherwise traveling all the way around something, especially the world.

city–state: a city and its surrounding area, which rules itself like a country.

civilization: a community of people that is advanced in art, science, and government.

classics: the study of ancient Greek and Latin literature, philosophy, and history.

commission: an instruction given to another person, such as an artist, for a piece of work.

component: a part of something.

compressed: pressed together very tightly, so something takes up less space.

cooperative: a business owned and run jointly by its members who also share the profits.

cosmography: the science of the general features of the universe, including Earth.

cryptography: the art of coding and decoding secret messages.

culture: the beliefs and way of life of a group of people, which can include religion, language, art, clothing, food, and holidays.

curriculum: the subjects included in a course of study.

custody: the guardianship or protective care of someone.

density: the amount of matter in a given space, or mass divided by volume.

dialectics: the art of investigating and discussing the truth of opinions.

dissect: to cut something apart to study what's inside.

distort: to make something look different from its normal shape.

doctorate: the highest advanced degree someone can receive in a field of study.

double cordiform: the projection of a map that looks like two heart shapes joined together.

dowry: property or money brought by a bride to her husband on their marriage.

duchy: the territory ruled by a duke or duchess.

elevation: a measurement of height above sea level.

elite: people with the most wealth or the highest status.

encrypt: to turn into code or a coded signal.

engineering: the use of science and math in the design and construction of machines and structures.

engraving: a type of printing in which the design is etched or drawn into the plate instead of the letters or design being raised on the plate.

entrepreneur: a person who organizes, manages, and takes on the risks associated with a business.

equine: relating to horseback riding.

equivalence principle: the theory that without air resistance, gravity makes all objects fall at the same rate of speed.

GLOSSARY

essential: necessary or extremely important.

façade: the face of a building, especially the front side that looks onto the street.

finance: to provide the money for a new business venture.

Flanders: a region that is now part of the Netherlands, France, and Belgium.

Flemish: relating to Flanders.

friar: a member of certain religious orders.

fruition: when an idea becomes reality.

geocentric: a model of the universe, now disproved, that the earth is the center of the solar system.

geographer: a person who studies the earth's surface and its people, plants, and animals.

geologic: having to do with geology, the science of the history of the earth.

goldsmithing: the job of working with gold.

gore: a triangular-shaped piece of cloth.

guild: an organization established to protect artists and merchants.

harmonious: free from disagreement or dissent.

heirs: people who inherit or have the right to inherit property.

heliocentrism: the idea that the sun is the center of the solar system.

heresy: having a belief that is not approved of by the church.

heretic: a person who disagrees with the traditional beliefs of a religion.

hospice: an inn for travelers, often run by a religious order.

humanism: a belief that human beings can improve themselves and their world through a rational approach to problem solving.

humanities: the study of literature, philosophy, and other arts.

hydrostatic balance: a balance that can accurately weigh objects both in air and water.

illuminator: someone who worked to add the finishing touches, such as color, to a manuscript.

immoral: something that goes against what is generally accepted as moral, or right.

inclination: a slant or slope.

inclined plane: a flat surface that connects a lower level to a higher level.

infectious: able to spread quickly from one person to others.

inheritance: money, property, or titles received at the death of a previous holder.

innovation: a new creation or a unique solution to a problem.

Inquisition: a court established by the Roman Catholic Church in the thirteenth century to try cases of heresy and other offenses against the church.

GLOSSARY

inquisitor: an officer of the Inquisition.

intellectual: involving serious thought.

inventor: a person who makes something new.

italic: a type of slanted writing.

Latin: the language of ancient Rome and its empire.

lift: an upward force.

literacy: the ability to read and write.

literature: written work such as poems, plays, and novels.

logic: the principle, based on math, that things should work together in an orderly way.

lute: a musical instrument that looks like a guitar but has a pear-shaped body.

martyr: a person who endures great suffering and death for his or her religious beliefs.

mass-produce: to manufacture large amounts of a product.

mass production: the production of a large quantity of goods, usually by machinery.

mechanical: done automatically or as if by machine, not by a person.

medieval: the Middle Ages, after the fall of the Roman Empire, from about 350 to 1450 CE.

mentor: a more experienced person who guides a younger or more inexperienced person.

Mercator's projection: a map on which the lines of latitude and longitude cross at right angles, and the areas farther from the equator appear larger.

merchant: a person who buys and sells goods for a profit.

Middle Ages: the period between the end of the Roman Empire and the beginning of the Renaissance, from about 350 to 1450 CE. It is also called the Medieval Era.

mint: a place where money is coined (made), commonly under state authority.

molten: melted, typically by very great heat.

monopoly: complete control of something, such as a service or product.

nautical: relating to ships, shipping, sailors, or navigation on a body of water.

navigation: planning and following a route.

Northwest Passage: a sea route along the northern coast of North America, connecting the Atlantic and Pacific Oceans.

notary: a person authorized to draw up or certify documents to show that they are authentic.

optical: anything connected to light.

ornithopter: an aircraft that must flap its wings to fly.

Palestine: an ancient region that borders on the Mediterranean's eastern coast and extends east of the Jordan River.

pamphlet: a small booklet or leaflet.

papacy: the system of government in the Catholic Church headed by the pope.

papier-mâché: a strong but light molding material made from paper pulp mixed with glue and other substances.

paternal: related to someone through their father.

patron: a person who gives financial support to a person or organization.

peasant: a farmer who lived on and farmed land owned by his lord.

pendulum: a weight hung from a fixed point that swings back and forth.

penmanship: the quality or style of handwriting.

perpendicular: when an object forms a right angle with another object.

perspective: the technique of drawing or painting a scene so objects in it appear to have depth and distance.

philosophy: the study of truth, wisdom, the nature of reality, and knowledge.

physics: the science of how matter and energy work together.

pigment: a substance that gives color to something.

pilgrim: a traveler on a journey to a holy place.

plague: a deadly infectious disease carried by rats and mice that can spread to humans.

plumb line: a line with a weight at one end that is used to measure depth or find out if something is vertical.

platen: the plate in a small printing press that presses the paper against the type.

polyalphabetic: a cipher based on several substitutions.

polyhedron: a shape with many sides.

printing press: a machine that presses inked type onto paper.

profit: the money made in a business after all the expenses have been paid.

prolific: producing many works.

proportion: the balanced relationships between parts of a whole.

propulsion: pushing or moving an object forward.

prototype: a model of something that allows engineers to test their idea.

rational: based on reason or logic.

Reformation: a religious movement beginning in 1500 that rejected the Catholic pope and established the Protestant churches.

relief: a work of art with raised figures or designs that stand out from the background.

Renaissance: the period in European history between the 1300s and 1700, which was marked by dramatic social, political, artistic, and scientific change.

GLOSSARY

resource: something that people can use.

sacred: highly valued and important.

satellite: an object that orbits the earth, or that orbits the sun or another planet.

sculpture: the art of making two- or three-dimensional representations of forms, especially by carving wood or stone or by casting metal or plaster.

seamstress: someone who earns a living by sewing.

secretary: an official who works to organize and conduct correspondence.

sector: a tool that measures the angular distance between two bodies.

specific gravity: the ratio of the density of one substance to the density of another substance (such as water) taken as a standard when both the densities are weighed in air.

suburb: where people live near a city.

survey: to use math to measure angles, distances, and elevations on Earth's surfaces.

terrestrial: related to land.

theology: the study of religion or ideas about religion.

topographical: having to do with the features of the land, such as mountains.

type: a rectangular block that has a raised number or letter from which an inked print is made.

Vatican: an independent state, located within Rome, which serves as the headquarters for the pope.

vellum: fine paper made from the skin of a calf.

RESOURCES

BOOKS

- Feinstein, Stephen. *Johannes Gutenberg: The Printer Who Gave Words to the World.* Enslow Publishers Inc., 2008.

- Heinrichs, Ann. *Gerardus Mercator: Father of Modern Mapmaking.* Capstone, 2007.

- Hilliam, Rachel. *Galileo Galilei: Father of Modern Science.* Rosen Publishing Group, 2005.

- *Inventors and Inventions, Volume* 4. Marshall Cavendish, 2008.

- Osborne, Mary Pope, and Natalie Pope Boyce. *Leonardo da Vinci: A Nonfiction Companion to Magic Tree House Merlin Mission #10: Monday with a Mad Genius.* Random House Books for Young Readers, 2009.

- Panchyk, Richard. *Galileo for Kids: His Life and Ideas.* Chicago Review Press, 2005.

RESOURCES

WEBSITES

- **Galileo Galilei: BBC**
  *bbc.co.uk/science/space/solarsystem/
  scientists/galileo_galilei*

- **The Humanities And Education: Kids Past**
  kidspast.com/world-history/the-renaissance-italy

- **Leonardo da Vinci 1452-1519: BBC**
  bbc.co.uk/science/leonardo

- **Printing And Thinking: Annenberg Learner**
  learner.org/interactives/renaissance/printing

- **Renaissance: Kids Discover**
  online.kidsdiscover.com/unit/renaissance

- **Renaissance Civilization: BBC**
  *bbc.co.uk/schools/gcsebitesize/history/shp/
  middleages/earlymoderncivilisationrev1.shtml*

QR CODE GLOSSARY

PAGE 6: youtube.com/watch?v=MD_wZLpaVPg

PAGE 9: youtube.com/watch?v=QAad2XcD2R4

PAGE 20: intratext.com/X/LAT0192.htm

PAGE 21: loc.gov/exhibits/bibles/the-gutenberg-bible.html

PAGE 29: khanacademy.org/humanities/ap-art-history/
early-europe-and-colonial-americas/renaissance-art-europe-ap/v/alberti-palazzo-rucellai

PAGE 30: loc.gov/resource/cph.3c10281

PAGE 32: youtube.com/watch?v=SPeWOYWLVvE

PAGE 53: khanacademy.org/humanities/renaissance-reformation/
high-ren-florence-rome/leonardo-da-vinci/v/leonardo-anatomist

PAGE 57: bl.uk/turning-the-pages/?id=cb4c06b9-02f4-49af-80ce-540836464a46&type=book

PAGE 58: historystack.com/17_Most_Amazing_Leonardo_da_Vinci's_Drawings

PAGE 58: works-words.com/NSM-WIKI/WP/wordpress/wiki/skydiving/
giants-of-the-vast-sky/sky-people-of-note/adrian-nicholas-replica-da-vinci-flight-tested

PAGE 59: mos.org/leonardo/activities/mirror-writing

PAGE 67: hcl.harvard.edu/libraries/maps/exhibits/mercator/terrestrial/index_nav4.html

PAGE 68: hcl.harvard.edu/libraries/maps/exhibits/mercator/celestial/index.html

PAGE 73: google.com/doodles/gerardus-mercators-503rd-birthday

PAGE 76: bl.uk/collection-items/mercator-atlas-of-europe

PAGE 79: youtube.com/watch?v=5SnR-eOS6Ic

PAGE 87: youtube.com/watch?v=3YiAqgEh8SY

PAGE 88: youtube.com/watch?v=4mTsrRZEMwA

PAGE 91: college.cengage.com/history/world/bulliet/earth_peoples/2e/students/primary/galileo.htm

PAGE 96: youtube.com/watch?v=E43-CfukEgs

INDEX

INDEX